STANDARDS
IN PRACTICE
GRADES K-2

STANDARDS IN PRACTICE GRADES K-2

LINDA K. CRAFTON

National Council of Teachers of English

1111 W. Kenyon Road, Urbana, Illinois

61801–1096

Manuscript Editor: Jennifer Wilson
Production Editor: Michael Greer
Cover and Interior Design: R. Maul
Cover Photograph and Interior Photographs on pp. 51
and 105: Thompson-McClellan Photography

NCTE Stock Number 46910-3050

It is the policy of NCTE in its journals and other publications to provide a forum for the open
discussion of ideas concerning the content and the teaching of English and the language arts.
Publicity accorded to any particular point of view does not imply endorsement by the Executive
Committee, the Board of Directors, or the membership at large, except in announcements of
policy, where such endorsement is clearly specified.

Although every attempt is made to ensure accuracy at the time of publication,
NCTE cannot guarantee that published electronic mail addresses are current.

Library of Congress Cataloging-in-Publication Data

Crafton, Linda K.
    Standards in practice, grades K–2 / Linda K. Crafton
      p. cm.
    Includes bibliographical references.
    "NCTE stock number, 46910-3050"–T.p. verso.
    ISBN 0-8141-4691-0
    1. Language arts (Primary)–United States. 2. Language arts
(Primary)–Standards–United States. I. National Council of
Teachers of English. II. Title.
LB1529.U5C73 1996
372.6–dc20   95-26593
                                              CIP

FOREWORD

This book is one of four in the NCTE Standards in Practice series. The idea for this series grew out of requests from many teachers around the country who participated in the development of the NCTE/IRA standards and who asked if we could publish a book or a series of books that would illustrate what the standards might look like in actual classrooms at different grade levels.

This request was both inviting and challenging. Because one of the main goals of NCTE is to support classroom teachers, providing a series of books that would help define the standards seemed like the sort of thing we should do—and it is the type of thing, we like to think, we do quite well. At the same time, there were many challenges in developing these books. We wondered: Could we do it? What might these books look like? What standards would we use? How important would uniformity and consistency be among the books in the series?

The four authors and I spent time exploring these questions and it soon became evident that the development of this series was, perhaps, both simpler and even more important than we had originally thought. We decided that if we asked English language arts teachers who were doing interesting and challenging work in their classrooms to reflect in writing on their practices and to tell us their stories, the standards would be there, already at work in students' learning. After all, the English language arts standards did emerge from those practices that our membership and the IRA membership said they valued most. The standards do not stand above and apart from the practices of actual classroom teachers, or dictate to them—rather they represent what those teachers and the many others involved in English language arts education agree is the best and most productive current thinking about teaching and learning. We also decided that each book in the series did not have to follow the same generic format. What each book should do instead is tell its own story and use the format that best fits and supports the story or stories being told.

All of us agreed that we wanted the books in this series to be stories or rich illustrations of classroom practice. Stories, we thought, would allow the writers to capture the rich and complex activities of teaching and learning and, in addition, would illustrate the interconnectedness of the English language arts and of the standards themselves. We also wanted our readers to see how teachers create contexts as well as learning experiences. We thought it was important for the readers to experience both the struggles *and* the successes teachers and students encounter. And we hoped that the stories would make explicit the importance of the teacher as researcher. We believe the standards are dynamic in nature and will change and improve only if teachers actively and deliberately interrogate their own practice—learning and growing from their professional and classroom experiences.

In these four books we meet caring teachers who meet all our most challenging criteria for teaching and learning. They are women and men who think deeply about the quality of life and intellectual growth they provide for their students. Some of the teachers we meet in the series are new to the profession and are trying out ideas for the first time. Others have been teaching for many years but, as always, are reflecting on and questioning some of their practices, and in their stories we see them making changes. All of them, whether they are teaching five-year-olds or eighteen-year-olds, whether they themselves have been teaching for five or for eighteen or more years, put students' learning at the center of their curricula and engage their students in challenging, authentic experiences. By presenting an array of classroom portraits, these volumes clearly show that standards are always present in good practice and that there is no one way for the standards to be realized.

I want to commend the teachers and students who are featured in this series and the writers who told their stories. They have opened their classrooms to us and let us look in, and, in so doing, they have enriched our understandings of what matters most in the English language arts.

–*Karen Smith*
Associate Executive Director
National Council of Teachers of English

CONTENTS

NCTE/IRA Standards for the English Language Arts..............................viii

Introduction..x

1. For the Love of Literature 2

2. For the Love of Writing..12

3. Real-World Learning and Emergent Literacy.................................28

4. Language, Literature, and Multicultural Understanding...................50

5. Interest Groups and Evaluation:
   Children in Charge of Their Learning...66

6. Inquiry and the Iditarod..84

7. Making Meaning in Reading, Writing, Art, Music, and Drama 98

8. Narrative Writing:
   Toward a "Real Kid" Report Card...110

Author 121

NCTE/IRA
STANDARDS FOR THE
ENGLISH LANGUAGE ARTS

The vision guiding these standards is that all students must have the opportunities and resources to develop the language skills they need to pursue life's goals and to participate fully as informed, productive members of society. These standards assume that literacy growth begins before children enter school as they experience and experiment with literacy activities—reading and writing, and associating spoken words with their graphic representations. Recognizing this fact, these standards encourage the development of curriculum and instruction that make productive use of the emerging literacy abilities that children bring to school. Furthermore, the standards provide ample room for the innovation and creativity essential to teaching and learning. They are not prescriptions for particular curriculum or instruction.

Although we present these standards as a list, we want to emphasize that they are not distinct and separable; they are, in fact, interrelated and should be considered as a whole.

1. Students read a wide range of print and nonprint texts to build an understanding of texts, of themselves, and of the cultures of the United States and the world; to acquire new information; to respond to the needs and demands of society and the workplace; and for personal fulfillment. Among these texts are fiction and nonfiction, classic and contemporary works.

2. Students read a wide range of literature from many periods in many genres to build an understanding of the many dimensions (e.g., philosophical, ethical, aesthetic) of human experience.

3. Students apply a wide range of strategies to comprehend, interpret, evaluate, and appreciate texts. They draw on their prior experience, their interactions with other readers and writers, their knowledge of word meaning and other texts, their word identification strategies, and their understanding of textual features (e.g., sound-letter correspondence, sentence structure, context, graphics).

4. Students adjust their use of spoken, written, and visual language (e.g., conventions, style, vocabulary) to communicate effectively with a variety of audiences and for different purposes.

5. Students employ a wide range of strategies as they write and use different writing process elements appropriately to communicate with different audiences for a variety of purposes.

6. Students apply knowledge of language structure, language conventions (e.g., spelling and punctuation), media techniques, figurative language, and genre to create, critique, and discuss print and nonprint texts.

7. Students conduct research on issues and interests by generating ideas and questions, and by posing problems. They gather, evaluate, and synthesize data from a variety of sources (e.g., print and nonprint texts, artifacts, people) to communicate their discoveries in ways that suit their purpose and audience.

8. Students use a variety of technological and informational resources (e.g., libraries, databases, computer networks, video) to gather and synthesize information and to create and communicate knowledge.

9. Students develop an understanding of and respect for diversity in language use, patterns, and dialects across cultures, ethnic groups, geographic regions, and social roles.

10. Students whose first language is not English make use of their first language to develop competency in the English language arts and to develop understanding of content across the curriculum.

11. Students participate as knowledgeable, reflective, creative, and critical members of a variety of literacy communities.

12. Students use spoken, written, and visual language to accomplish their own purposes (e.g., for learning, enjoyment, persuasion, and the exchange of information).

INTRODUCTION

The *Standards for the English Language Arts* have been carved out over many long months; the process has been filled with passionate conversations from multiple and diverse audiences. Thousands of educators, researchers, parents, and others around the country have engaged in extended discussions to help articulate the best of what we know and practice in the name of language learning. The final document signals the beginning of new conversations. This time the voices will belong to communities of schools and districts around the country who will read, reflect, and talk about the meaning of this vision for their particular school: Is it dramatically different from what is already in place? What do these ideas mean for increasing the quality of education for the students in *this* school? In *this* unique community? The authors of the English language arts document speak of teachers "engaging" with the standards. It is their hope, and mine, that these statements of what students should know and be able to do in the English language arts will be viewed as a point of departure rather than a final destination.

Just as the development of these standards occurred as the result of exchanges among various stakeholders, their implementation should follow a similar process. There are obvious voices that must be heard: teachers, administrators, and parents. These will be serious, well-intentioned voices with predictably diverse interpretations of the standards and the best ways to handle them. But these are, once again, adult voices. Adult standards, produced by adults with an eye toward adult implementation. Ultimately, it is children who are the intended recipients; it is they who must deal with our goals and come to own them. Now it is imperative that we find ways to pull them into the dialogue as well. In the end, these standards belong to them or they belong to no one.

Finding ways to increase student ownership of learning in the classroom has been a primary goal for learning- and learner-centered educators for some time. The standards should be seen as another opportunity to strengthen this critical dimension of thinking: Students can be helped to understand and shape the expectations they are to meet. They can ask, as we have, What is it that we value above all? What comprises a rich and meaningful learning experience for *me*?

Does it make sense to engage kindergartners, first graders, and second graders in a conversation about something as adult as standards? In classrooms around the country, children are already talking about standards every day: They proudly announce a new strategy that helps them comprehend a piece of literature; they respond to one another's drafts during writing workshops (and then ask the author if it was helpful); they practice repeatedly for a Readers' Theater performance until they judge it ready for a public audience; they write recommendations for books they have read and tell specifically the qualities they like or don't like; they carefully select artifacts and determine why they belong in portfolios; and they brainstorm simple rubrics and then use evaluative thinking to guide the development of presentations and revisions of their work.

These wonderful reflections and self-evaluations take place in classrooms where standards are not the center, not the goal, not ends in themselves. At the center of these classrooms are children and meaning and language. Within and because of these purposeful, ongoing experiences, serious talk about quality and proficiency occur. And it is within these experiences that standards emerge and interact in complex ways.

The teaching and learning stories that you will read here evolved with teachers focusing first and foremost on good teaching and on improving the quality of their instruction. These educators define good teaching as decision making grounded in current knowledge about children, learning, and literacy. They define good teaching as pedagogy that recognizes, respects, and builds from individual language strengths and experiences. They, like the *Standards* contributors, see students in their classrooms as diverse, never deficient: "If we learn to recognize and value a variety of student abilities in the language arts and then build on these strengths, we can make it possible for all students to attain high standards. Some will reach the standards quickly and others more slowly, but we believe all students can reach them" (p. 9).

The teachers in this book also believe that good teaching is about continual change and readjustment, not static application of someone else's ideas. These are reflective teachers at varying levels of experience exploring different dimensions of primary-grade teaching. Their explorations are characterized by reflection, professional reading and study, and conversations with other teachers who have similar goals. The parts of their classrooms and themselves that they share with you in this book represent a range of issues that confront every kindergarten, first- and second-grade teacher in our country: reading and writing processes, strategies and skills, integration, inquiry, phonics, literature-based reading, restructuring beliefs, increasingly diverse classrooms, parent education, technology, inclusion, and multiple forms of communication, among many others.

The teachers highlighted here share common beliefs about teaching and learning. Their stories are undergirded by a set of shared commitments (Edelsky, 1994) that individually and collectively inform their practice and determine their responses to students. Within this set of commitments, education for democracy is the umbrella principle. As educators, we must be committed to democratic principles in our classrooms, especially those that relate to power, equity, and meaningful participation. These principles are what drive Elliott to work harder at dealing with gender bias and seeking an increased voice for marginalized ethnic groups in his multicultural classroom; democratic issues are why Marcia promotes social responsibility and critical reading in her second-grade classroom; democracy at work in the classroom pushes Kathy to include the learner perspective in her latest version of a transformed report card.

Shared Commitments

The set of shared commitments that define the practice, encourage the growth, and stimulate the questions of the teachers in this book include:

- commitment to education for democracy
- commitment to valuing diversity
- commitment to meaning-centered curriculum
- commitment to choice
- commitment to developing critical, strategic thought
- commitment to teaching the underlying processes of literacy
- commitment to collaboration
- commitment to story
- commitment to whole-to-part teaching
- commitment to authentic experience

(See Edelsky, 1994)

Like the teachers profiled in this book, we must see standards development as an opportunity to expand thinking and curriculum, not to reduce them. Our new guidelines for the English language arts can help us help our students forge a new language and an altered way of looking at themselves as readers, writers, and thinkers. But it must be accomplished within the context of purposeful, authentic engagements. We can watch and trust that these standards will emerge if we maintain a steady focus on what we know about children, development, process, and learning.

Implementing the National Standards

It is likely that the English language arts standards will be implemented in ways we can't even imagine at this point. But some of these ways will result in stronger, child-focused classrooms while others can only lead to fragmented instruction where children are shoved aside in favor of discrete statements about what learners should do and know. One dangerous path would be to start with an individual standard statement and compile a list of activities related to that goal. It's hard to imagine that a curriculum developed in this way could move beyond an activity level. Indeed, the authors state that the standards derive from a "vision of a more challenging future." As a profession, we have moved beyond the generation of curriculum from a predetermined set of learning statements. As emphasized above, curriculum is most effective when it begins with beliefs and learners, and makes meaning and communication central. The writing of the standards and this book was guided by an unflagging belief in the learner's critical role, "whose goals and interests drive the processes of learning" (*Standards*, p. 1).

With learners and meaning as the pivotal point, we have a chance of seeing the standards emerge authentically within the language/literacy experience itself. If our focus becomes the standards themselves, then we have a significantly decreased possibility of realizing our deeper goals and commitments.

Consider beginning the standards implementation with a thoughtful review of assumptions about teaching and learning, examples of best practice, or one of the stories in this book. Wherever you begin, invite other educators to think with you. Not only are you likely to find that the conversations are the best part of the implementation, but that you are actively bringing to life our most heartfelt professional standard: engagement that results in personal change.

More than anything, we hope that these standards, this book, and the generosity of these teachers sharing their experiences will help you move along significantly in your learning journey. What is our vision of a stronger American education system? What is our hope for primary classrooms that not only respect children but prepare them to meet the challenges of the future? We invite you to read on.

References

Edelsky, C. (1994). Education for democracy. *Language Arts, 71*(4), 252–257.
Standards for the English language arts. (1996). Urbana, IL: National Council of Teachers of English/International Reading Association.

DEDICATION

This book is dedicated to all the K–2 teachers around the country who strive every day to reach new standards in their teaching and who help students develop and achieve their own high standards.

A special dedication to the primary teachers in this book who generously shared their classrooms, writing, and professional thinking with me on incredibly short notice. Thank you Kathy Egawa, Sue Smeaton, Pat Riordan, Lynn White, Mary Vondrak, Marcia Sostrin, Elliott Cady, and, especially, Penny Silvers.

With thanks to Karen Smith, for the invitation and constant support of my work and thinking over the past few years; to Kathy Short, Marti Hancock, and Janet Files, for the time and thoughtful energy which helped me uncover and focus on the key issues; and to Michael Greer, my capable editor, for sharing a heartfelt appreciation of the teachers, the children, and the stories.

CHAPTER ONE

FOR THE LOVE OF LITERATURE

Before reading, consider . . .
- *The ways you talk about books, movies, or TV shows with your friends.*
- *Three of your all-time favorite books: Why do you remember them? What was significant about them to you?*
- *How are you encouraging talk about books in your classroom?*

It was January, and Eileen, only three years away from retirement, had been telling her friends for some time that she was suffering from "severe teacher burnout": "I was bored and I felt my first graders were probably bored, too, maybe more than I wanted to admit." For all of her professional life, Eileen had taught reading using a basal series. Her students were ability-grouped from the first week of school, and she believed that almost all of the children who passed through her class left it with a solid base of skills for reading. She wasn't sure, however, how many of them left the first grade on their way to becoming life-long readers, or would love to read, as she did. Of course, there were always the obvious ones in the "low" group; she and her colleagues talked often about how tough they were to pull in, and she had recognized long ago that much of her time with this group was spent disciplining instead of teaching. These young readers were definitely not developing a great affection for books. In fact, they steered away from them at all costs. That made sense to her; reading was just too much of a struggle for them.

All of this created a heartfelt sadness in her. She thought about her own love of books, the book club she had belonged to for years, and the wonderful conversations she always looked forward to. It was her concern for this affective side of reading and her need for change that led her to consider a literature-based reading program for her classroom.

Eileen's district was fairly traditional, but her school's principal was generally open to new ideas. Eileen went to her with a proposal to try teaching reading with literature. "It'll be an experiment," she said. The principal asked how she planned to do it. Eileen had belonged to her local reading council for many years, attended local reading conferences, and received professional journals.

Each of these sources had promoted literature-based reading for some time, so she had some ideas. She told her principal she wanted to start slowly and take it a step at a time, with a five-day structure that she felt would provide a solid base as she explored the idea. On Mondays, she would allow the students to choose which books they would like to read and group them according to interest; they would review vocabulary for each set and have time to read independently. Tuesdays would serve as reading days. On Wednesdays and Thursdays, she would meet individually with each group to discuss the literature (about 30 minutes each); the groups not meeting would complete skills and phonics worksheets and read library books. On Fridays, they would exercise creative expression skills in art. Her general morning schedule, then, would include twenty minutes of journal writing (including sharing), one hour of literature and skill work, recess, and her usual read-aloud time before lunch. Eileen's principal gave her the go-ahead, with a request that she keep her posted.

Eileen knew she would need multiple copies of books to get started, and discussed the prospects of buying them with her principal. In the meantime, Eileen decided that the best way to quickly get multiple copies would be to try the public and school libraries. Since the groups would be heterogeneous, she needed to be careful about the selections in terms of readability. While looking through the available literature, it occurred to her that fairy tales might be a logical place to start. At the beginning of the school year, she had invited her children to retell the fairy tales they knew to each other, to her, and to the class. The retellings had been such a success that she'd asked the children to dramatize the stories, and this was another big hit. She knew that *Little Red Riding Hood, Cinderella, Jack and the Beanstalk,* and *Rapunzel* would be manageable reading for almost all of the children, and there was certainly enough "meat" in these stories to give them something to talk about—and besides, the libraries would surely have multiple copies of these popular tales.

She introduced the idea on Monday. "We're going to start reading real books during reading time from now on." There were cheers from the peanut gallery. "I have four that you can choose from, so listen carefully, and then I'll ask you to write down your top two choices." They did, and the first groups were formed. Eileen had selected difficult words from each story, and she reviewed them with the groups. The remaining time was used for silent reading. Eileen kept a watchful eye and gave help as it was needed. "Tomorrow I'll start with one group so we all have a chance to talk about our stories. Be sure to bring your best ideas." Several children who had not finished asked to take their books home that afternoon.

The first discussions were disastrous. Not only did her students not offer their *best* ideas, they offered almost *no* ideas. Eileen was left to do most of the talking. She had thought carefully about how to begin and had settled on, "What did you think of the story?" "It was good." "I liked it." Then she tried, "What did you like?" "The wolf." "When Jack had to run down the beanstalk." "When Cinderella went to the ball." She felt like she was back to teaching the basal material.

She did, however, run into a parent in the hall at the end of the week: "You know, Donald really liked being able to choose his book this week, and he wanted to make sure it was all read so he would be ready to 'talk.' Do you plan to keep doing that?" There *was* some enthusiasm from the students! She needed to think more about the nature of these discussions—there must be some trick she was missing. Eileen knew that one experience wasn't enough for anyone to develop skill in an area, but still, she had hoped for more.

A Few Good Picture Books for Starting Literature Discussions

Aardema, V. (1975). *Why mosquitoes buzz in people's ears*. New York: Dial.

Bunting, E. (1991). *Fly away home*. Boston: Clarion.

Carle, E. (1977). *The grouchy ladybug*. New York: Crowell.

Cooney, B. (1982). *Miss Rumphius*. New York: Viking.

De Paola, T. (1975). *Strega nona*. Englewood Cliffs, NJ: Prentice-Hall.

Galdone, P. (1970). *The three little pigs*. New York: Clarion.

Hazen, B. (1979). *Tight times*. New York: Viking.

Kroll, V. (1992). *Masai and I*. New York: Simon & Schuster.

Mills, L. (1991). *The rag coat*. Boston: Little, Brown & Company.

Rylandt, C. (1985). *The relatives came*. New York: Bradbury Press.

Sendak, M. (1963). *Where the wild things are*. New York: Harper & Row.

Steig, W. (1987). *Sylvester and the magic pebble*. New York: Simon & Schuster.

Van Allsburg, C. (1981). *Jumanji*. Boston: Houghton Mifflin.

Viorst, J. (1975). *The tenth good thing about Barney*. New York: Atheneum/Macmillan.

Waber, B. (1972). *Ira sleeps over*. Boston: Houghton Mifflin.

Yashima, T. (1955). *Crow boy*. New York: Viking.

Zolotow, C. (1972). *William's doll*. New York: Harper & Row.

Eileen spent the weekend buried in her professional journals and talking with a longtime friend who taught first grade in another district. Her friend had been using literature one day each week during reading time, but she had not tried small group discussions, because she really didn't think six-year-olds were up to it. The professional literature told a different story, and Eileen believed the potential was there—six-year-olds had astonished her too many times during her career for her to continue underestimating them. Didn't any of these teachers have problems when they started, though? Surely their students didn't engage in sophisticated conversation from the very beginning. Eileen decided to call a professor she'd had many years ago for a reading class; even then, this teacher educator had advocated the use of literature in elementary classrooms.

The phone call turned out to be more than worth the effort. Primarily, it confirmed many of her initial decisions: allowing the children to choose which books to study was critical in getting these groups to work; four to six children per group was usually a good number; and fairy tales were indeed reasonable places to start. Her mentor suggested she shorten the time with each group (15 to 20 minutes) and meet with them two or three times each week. Then she asked Eileen to describe the discussions in detail. Eileen related how she had asked what she thought was a good, open-ended question, but got little response. She explained how the students had commented briefly and said nothing else; the silence had made her nervous, so she'd asked another question. It was downhill from there.

There was laughter on the other end of the line, and Eileen wondered what was so funny. "I remember feeling that way, too," her mentor said. "If there was a moment's silence, then I felt it was my job to fill it up, but when I did, I ended up doing all the talking—*and* thinking! One of the things you have to learn is to simply wait. These kids have become so dependent on us to control the discussion with questions that it sometimes takes them a while to realize we want *them* to initiate the talk. Try telling them beforehand that you want them to come with one idea from the story that they thought was really important; they can use a bookmark as a reminder or write the page number or idea down so they won't forget, but it's their responsibility to do that before they come to the group. Let me know how it goes."

Eileen decided to recycle the fairy tales and give it one more try. She organized the groups again based on new reading choices, explained what she wanted them to do, reviewed vocabulary words once more, and gave them a block of time to read.

The next morning, she reminded the two groups that she planned to meet with that each student needed to come to the discussion group with a related idea that he or she felt was important. Later, she held her breath and called her first group: *Little Red Riding Hood*. She started by telling them that she had talked too much the last time and that the reason they were having these literature groups was for them to tell what *they* were thinking. She really wanted to know what was on their minds. Who would start? Gina's hand was up in a flash: "I think it's important that Red Riding Hood shared her food with her grandmother. It's important to share." Gina was sitting next to Eileen, and as she spoke, she had her face turned up, staring at Eileen with intense brown eyes. The little girl continued to look at her expectantly. Suddenly Eileen realized that Gina was waiting to hear whether her idea was right or not. Was sharing *really* the most important thing in the story? Eileen chose her words carefully: "Thank you, Gina, for being the first one to share what you think. Does anyone else think something different?" There was a flurry, and except for one girl who remained silent throughout, everyone contributed something from a slightly varied perspective. When the talk died down at different points, Eileen simply leaned back and waited.

That night she called her mentor again. This time she excitedly described a halting but relatively fluent conversation where most of the students shared their interpretations. She also described the fun. Her mentor's response helped to clarify the thinking that had occurred: "Boy, Gina really set the tone for that group, didn't she? Not only did she tell you what she thought was significant, but she seemed to tie it to her own life. I'll bet sharing is what her parents are talking about at home, and maybe you are at school, too. You might want to try asking them to actively think of ways to connect the stories to their lives."

Eileen did just that, and for many weeks, she sat back and listened to her first graders talk about what was important to them, what they liked, and how the story made them feel. She settled into a listener role with an occasional open-ended question, usually "Why do you think that's important?" or a request to clarify. One day, however, a group was reading a book she particularly enjoyed. She had felt until then that she shouldn't give her own opinions or interpretations, but with this book, she had a strong response and wanted to share what was important to *her*. She told the group how she felt, and noticed immediately that they were strong enough now to accept her idea as only one possibility. She also noticed how much better it felt to be an active participant than to be a monitoring sideliner.

That weekend, looking through professional materials on literature discussion, she reread an article called "Entertaining a Text." The issue of the teacher's role in literature discussion took on new meaning when she read Karen Smith's statement: "Because I think this idea of sharing perspective versus questioning is so important, I often ask myself, 'What would I do if I were sitting among adult friends?'"

Of course! Eileen's own book club experiences and love of literature had strongly influenced her desire to try literature discussions, but she had not consciously considered *how* she participated in the lively talk. What *did* she do in her book club conversations? Two things came to mind quickly: She always stated what she thought was the primary message, and she often critiqued the author's writing (her favorite response was to discuss character development). Another realization hit her: she never, ever sat back and said nothing. And she

Literature Discussions

1. Several pieces of literature should be selected by the teacher, the students, or both. These are introduced to the class by giving short book talks and then making the books available for the students to browse through. For young children, the teacher may read each choice aloud to the class.

2. Students join a Literature Discussion by signing up on a chart for a certain piece of literature or by having students mark their first and second choices on a piece of paper; the teacher then forms the groups. Groups should have 4-5 members.

3. Students read the literature and meet to discuss the book. Students can read the entire piece before coming to the group discussion or they can read the literature as they discuss it. If the group meets to discuss as they read, they meet for a more intensive discussion of the entire book when it is finished.

Literature discussions usually last anywhere from two days to a week, depending on the length of the book and the depth of the discussion about the book. Often, only half of the class is involved in an intensive discussion at one time, and the others are doing choice reading, literature response activities (murals, dioramas, pictures, paintings, papier-mâché, collage, sculpture, mobiles, posters, interviews, research of the setting of the book or the life of the author). If multiple copies are not available, picture books can be easily shared.

This description adapted from Short, K., & Harste, J. (1988). *Creating classrooms for authors.* Portsmouth, NH: Heinemann.

never quizzed her friends with "thoughtful" questions. It was an insight of major proportion. Finally, here was the thing that had been making her so uncomfortable: It didn't feel right to hear only what her students thought and to probe them occasionally, because she had a more active role to play. This idea of active participation felt more like "real" teaching to her, and she was relieved by this discovery.

Eileen's literature discussions continued throughout the year, and so did her reading and conversations with her mentor. Her principal found some funding for books, but Eileen usually tracked most of them down in various libraries or bought them herself. She also learned to use her children's book club money to buy multiple copies. One simple method she found was to have a group choose an author or illustrator to discuss—that way, they could read two or three different books by that author or illustrator within the same group. She also found that reading a book aloud and then giving time for discussion worked well.

Read-aloud time changed its character entirely. When she was reading to her children, she now encouraged dialogue, knowing that the more secure they felt here, the more they would risk in the small-group setting. She noticed more and more that her children engaged in "connected talk"—one child would make an observation, then another would respond or expand. She also observed that as the children's individual and collaborative meanings changed in quality, so did their art.

Eileen stayed with her basic five-day structure throughout the first year of her "experiment," but during the fall of the second year, she began to ask students to sign up for discussions when their groups were finished reading, and she varied the number of times she met with each group, depending on the depth and direction of the discussion. During the year, students began recommending literature to her for discussion. Each time this happened, she felt one step closer to her love-of-literature goal. She also reread *Grand Conversations* that year and was affirmed in her belief that literary elements can indeed

---

Author or Illustrator Study

When students take an in-depth look at an author or illustrator, they can begin to see writing and art as processes of thinking and decision making. Studying one author or illustrator should be filled with questions and explorations regarding the different strategies and styles that writers and illustrators use to communicate meaning. As students become more familiar with varying styles and structures in art and writing, they often experiment with these in their own work. They also bring an expanded knowledge base to the reading process that directly influences the kinds of predictions they can make when they are reading other works by the authors they have studied. Teachers can begin by introducing a particular author, setting up a display of many authors' books or asking students if they have a favorite author they would like to study.

Students and teachers should discuss alternative ways to study an author or illustrator; different students can be responsible for giving book talks on individual selections, students can read a few books and share favorite parts or illustrations, or everyone can read an entire collection and then come together for discussions with partners or small groups. Children may choose from a number of different authors and illustrators and come together in small groups based on choice and interest for the study.

Once an author or illustrator study is complete, students should extend from the work in some way. They may dramatize one selection; experiment with one artist's style and medium to illustrate a favorite part of one book or a student-written book; perform a Readers' Theater of one or more books studied; create a poster or display; or write to the author or illustrator with questions that weren't answered during the study, particularly about the writing or art process.

Resources

Commire, A. (Ed.). (1971–1990). *Something about the author: Facts & figures about contemporary authors & illustrators of books for young people.* (Vols. 1–61). Detroit: Gale.

Kingman, L. et al. (Eds.). (1978). *Illustrators of children's books: 1967–1976.* (Vol. 4). Boston: Horn Book.

Kingman, L. (Ed.). (1986). *Newbery & Caldecott medal books: 1976–1985.* Boston: Horn Book.

Scholastic Books Staff. (1994). *Meet the authors & illustrators.* New York: Scholastic.

---

mending literature to her for discussion. Each time this happened, she felt one step closer to her love-of-literature goal. She also reread *Grand Conversations* that year and was affirmed in her belief that literary elements can indeed enhance conversation. From that point on, she felt free to talk about character, plot, setting, and mood with her first graders.

During the third year, which was to be her retirement year, Eileen stopped selecting and reviewing vocabulary words before her students read, turning the responsibility over to them—they recorded difficult vocabulary words for themselves as they read and noted which ones were resolved during the discussions. Any words left that the students still felt were important were noted and predictions about their meaning were made. During this year, Eileen also began to understand that the phonics and skills worksheets were more of a stumbling block than a friendly companion to her love-of-literature goal. She read *Looking Closely: Exploring the Role of Phonics in One Whole Language Classroom* and saw that what the authors said about phonics development was true: "In the past (and, unfortunately, in the present in some classrooms at some times), phonics instruction has been mistakenly taught as an end in itself, with little or no connection to meaning." This book helped give form to a new belief that had been in the back of her mind for some time: Children develop an understanding of letter-sound relationships while using and learning language. She could see it in their journal writing, and now it was more visible to her in their reading.

The third year of the literature discussion experiment also brought two other pivotal events in her professional life. Her principal, who had not only been informed of the changes in Eileen's reading curriculum but who had also participated in a few literature discussions herself, invited Eileen to organize literature workshops for interested colleagues. And Eileen decided not to retire.

Dear Mrs. Gidot,

I have a book I think our class would really like. You should read it to our first grade class. The story is by Henry Wadwor Wadsworth and is called Hiawatha's Child Hood. It has good pictures and is a indan story.

Love, Gina

Reflective Commentary

Teaching is a personal journey, one that should go slowly and take time. Eileen's experience shows that our profession works best when it is filled with thoughtful examination, conversation, and reflection. She does indeed take her transition to literature "one step at a time," but the interesting point is that she had many years of reading, thinking, talking, and listening to others in preparation for that first step. Like all the underlying, invisible development that occurs

R. S. V. P.
Reader-Selected Vocabulary Procedure
John C. Stansell

1. Before students begin reading, explain that if they encounter any unknown words, they should mark those words with a check and then promptly resume reading.
2. At the end of the reading time, students are to look over what they have read and make some judgments about the words they have marked.
3. As students read, watch for those who may need a reminder or some encouragement to just mark and keep going.
4. When students have completed the reading, hand out copies of a reading activity sheet, which consists of a sheet of paper that has been divided into four columns headed:

WORDS I KNOW AFTER READING	IMPORTANT WORDS I'M NOT SURE ABOUT	MY BEST GUESS	REFERENCE

This sheet serves as a guide for evaluating the words students have marked and for discovering an effective strategy for handling unknown words.

5. Ask students to look back at the words they have marked, and to note first those words whose meanings they now know. These words are to be listed in the first column.
6. Ask students to examine the remaining words, whose meanings are unknown, and to judge whether the words are important in understanding the reading selection. If so, these words are listed at the top of the second column.
7. If some words seem less important, students may list them at the bottom of the second column under the heading, "Other Words I'm Not Sure About."
8. Students jot down what they think each word in column two means in the column labeled "My Best Guess."
9. Students use such references as dictionaries, textbooks, atlases, maps, globes, encyclopedias, other students, or a teacher to confirm their best guesses. As words are looked up, a check mark is placed in the "Reference" column when the student judges a guess to be on target. If a guess is incorrect, students enter the correct definition in the "Reference" column in their own words and note its relationship to their best guess.
10. When all the definitions have been verified, students choose one of the words on their lists. Without referring to the activity sheet, they explain to their classmates what the word means.
11. A follow-up discussion can help students realize that the "mark-it-and-keep-going" strategy of R.S.V.P. pays off in terms of learning new words in an efficient and natural way. Students can also understand that the words labeling key ideas occur repeatedly and in contexts that make these ideas clear, while word meanings that are not made clear by the total context are usually not critical to understanding the selection. By waiting to consult the dictionary or other references until they complete their reading, students will have a shorter list of unknown words; they will have at least some idea of a word's meaning and will be more apt to understand the dictionary entry.

This description adapted from D. J. Watson (Ed.), (1987). *Ideas and insights: Language arts in the elementary school.* Urbana, IL: National Council of Teachers of English.

before a child says his or her first word, Eileen had been consciously and unconsciously exploring some of the assumptions that guide skill-based or language-based teaching of reading. Two key transitional issues that emerge from her story (and are inextricably bound) are related to the role of the teacher and to the question of who has control of the discussion.

From the beginning, Eileen theorized that choice and responsibility were critical for authentic literature discussions. Theory-practice relationships, however, are not always self-evident. Through her own experiences with an adult book club, Eileen held a social view of thinking about and learning through literature—each month when she joined her friends for coffee, dessert, and book talk, she walked away with a different understanding than she'd had when she arrived. Together, she and her friends created new meanings and perspectives that no one person could have generated alone. She knew that control and responsibility for the discussion formed a shared dimension.

Eileen carried an inside-out view of what literature discussions were all about, but her initial efforts in the classroom were guided more by her past teaching experiences than by self-knowledge, a situation many teachers find themselves in as they move from one paradigm to another. Eileen experienced many of the same problems that other teachers do when they move from a basal teaching series to literature. Some approach the discussions either in too open-ended a manner (asking a question and then hoping the children will fill the void) or in a too restrictive, thought-controlling manner (asking question after question, desperately trying to get a "conversation" going, all the while shutting down the possibility) that many have termed "basalizing" the literature. Eileen's path moved from one extreme to the other until, in her third year, she settled into a role that is best described as demonstrator—her efforts developed a conscious focus on showing children how to genuinely talk about literature.

Gilles (1994) notes that another first-grade teacher's beginning literature study "emphasized mechanical aspects of reading rather than the making of meaning" (p. 501). She, too, moved her literature discussions forward so that the children had many opportunities to interpret what they read—an instructional expectation that immediately moves comprehension far beyond the literal level. Villaume and Worden (1993) discuss the developmental differences between students who are passive and those who actively contribute during literature discussions:

> If students engage in literature discussions in passive ways where they are expected only to provide the answers to questions posed by other people, their independent thinking about literature will reflect the same passivity. If they engage in literature discussions where all participants are expected to provide and elaborate on personal responses, literate voices will develop. (p. 463)

The emphasis here is on *teacher expectation*—readers who are *expected* to focus their cognitive energies on interpretation will learn to do so, both in and out of school. Over the last ten years, many teachers and researchers have shown us that primary children have no trouble with interpretive thought. In fact, they show a quick facility at contextualizing one experience to help them understand another (such as Gina's statement about sharing as the theme in *Little Red Riding Hood*). If we ask kindergartners or first graders to answer specific text-based questions, they will, and they will develop a high degree of skill in doing so. If, however, we ask them to interpret what they read and imbue it with personal meaning, this is the kind of thinking ability they will develop. These positions represent not only great differences in the quality of thinking being encouraged, they also represent two very different sets of teaching standards. What, then, do we want our children to learn to do?

Impressively, the teacher Gilles highlights, like Eileen, approached her continued implementation of literature discussion from a teacher research perspective: What are my questions? Where am I in my journey? What resources can I use to help? Both teachers, one a veteran of many years and one newer to the profession, relied on self-knowledge, informed observation, professional texts, conversations with other professionals, and ongoing reflection to transform their teaching.

Another gradual transition is apparent in Eileen's story—the slow integration of skills into the larger reading process. First, she gave up the prereading identification of difficult vocabulary and encouraged her students to handle this themselves during their reading. Then came skills and phonics worksheets as she came to believe that these were most effective when introduced at the point of need. In *Basal Readers: A Second Look*, (1994), Edelsky reminds us that exercise isn't always healthy and that there is no evidence to support the transfer of skills from practice situations to authentic ones (p. 21). Eileen's assistance during silent reading time became an opportunity to encourage the use of basic read-

ing strategies: predicting, rereading, and noticing the initial consonant and picture clues. This, too, highlights the increased responsibility her students assumed for every aspect of their learning. Just as important, every step toward integration was a step toward increased time to *just read,* a curricular component which is still missing in many language arts classrooms.

Many teachers turn to literature to try to instill in children the same love of books that they feel themselves, just as Eileen did. Jacobs (1965) gives four reasons for using literature:

1. It is a wonderful, constructive way to put in time.
2. Literature offers an escape from the routines of everyday life.
3. Literature raises the spirits when readers discover that other people have the same experiences.
4. Literature can give new meaning to many situations.

Peterson and Eeds (1990) discuss "grand conversations," and the best literature discussions certainly are. As Gilles (1994) points out, though, when teachers begin literature study in their own classrooms, the discussions may not be as sophisticated as others they have read about or as highly developed as they'd hoped they would be. Like Eileen, each of us struggles when we attempt to put something new into place. Literature-based teaching is no different—it is a complex practice. There is no reason to think that it will happen overnight, but it is worth the reflective struggle, because it moves our students closer to the kinds of authentic development, literate voices, and deep love of reading that we envision for them, which are all major "standards" from any perspective.

Note: These are shortened versions of the standards. The full text of the English language arts standards may be found on pages viii–ix.

What Key Standards Emerge and Interact in This Context?

Students read a range of print and nonprint texts. Students read and discussed in literature circles fairy tales, picture books, predictable books, nonfiction, and poetry. They learned to identify what was important to them in fiction and nonfiction and could share individual interpretations. They listened to book talks and made decisions about what books they would like to read.

Students read a wide range of literature. Eileen read aloud to her students every day, careful to include a range of genres from picture books to poetry. Her students selected from a range of literature and recommended a variety of fiction and nonfiction they wanted to read and discuss in literature groups. They learned to explore alternative perspectives in relation to the literature they chose to read.

Students apply a range of strategies. Through literature discussion and teacher facilitation, students discovered the value of making personal connections to the stories they read and learned to use their prior knowledge (personal experiences and other texts) to influence their thinking.

Students capitalized on their interactions with peers and the teacher to help them comprehend stories more deeply—they extended from each other's thinking, asked questions about different interpretations, and reread sections of text together.

Students selected and recorded ideas they wanted to talk about during literature discussion.

Students participate in a variety of literacy communities. Throughout the year, students belonged to a number of different literature discussion groups which were formed heterogeneously, based on interest. In these groups, they read, selected personally significant information, reflected on their own and others' interpretations, compared and critiqued published works, and recommended future books for discussion. Students also became members of larger, unknown literacy communities as they joined first graders across the country and around the world reading fairy tales and picture books. They were knowledgeable, contributing members of their own first-grade community, reading and sharing books independently and responding to those read aloud by the teacher. Many students reported reading to younger siblings and so created their own literacy groups.

Students use spoken, written, and visual language to accomplish their own purposes. Student literature recommendations often came from books they had purchased or checked out of the local library. Parents often reported to Eileen that their children were asking to go to the library, reading independently at home—and talking about their books.

References and Other Resources

Edelsky, C. (1994). Exercise isn't always healthy. In *Basal readers: A second look.* Katonah, NY: Richard C. Owen.

Gilles, C., Dickinson, J., McBride, C., & Vandover, M. (1994). Discussing our questions and questioning our discussions: Growing into literature study. *Language Arts, 71*(7): 499–508.

Jacobs, L. (Ed.). (1965). *Using literature with children.* New York: Teachers College Press.

Mills, H., O'Keefe, T., & Stephens, D. (1992). *Looking closely: Exploring the role of phonics in one whole language classroom.* Urbana, IL: National Council of Teachers of English.

Peterson, R., & Eeds, M. (1990). *Grand conversations: Literature groups in action.* Ontario, Canada: Scholastic.

Smith, K. (1990). Entertaining a text. In K. G. Short & K. M. Pierce (Eds.), *Talking about books.* Portsmouth, NH: Heinemann.

Villaume, S., & Worden, T. (1993). Developing literate voices: The challenge of whole language. *Language Arts, 70*(6): 462–468.

Chapter Two

For the Love of Writing

Before reading, consider . . .
- *One time when you have felt the power of writing in your life.*
- *Your beliefs about beginning writing.*
- *The reasons the children in your classroom write.*

Stavros's Masterpiece

On this special spring day, Stavros knew that he was going to share the five-page masterpiece he had been working on for some time in his first-grade classroom. He had shared his first draft with fellow students and read it to several "buddy readers" from the third-grade class, who frequently came to help with projects in his room. He had also read his story to the principal, who often stopped in during Writers' Workshop to help conference and listen to the students' stories. At exactly 10:15 A.M., the teacher, Bev Jones, gave a signal, and the class knew it was time to get out their writing folders to continue with their works in progress.

Stavros pulled out his completed story, a mystery called "The Lost Garage Door Opener." During workshop time, he put the finishing touches on his "published" copy (a final draft edited with the teacher or parent volunteers, carefully copied in the child's own handwriting, and "bound" together like a book), embellished the illustrations, and practiced reading it to two friends so it would sound smooth and interesting. He told his teacher when she stopped by to check on his progress, "I want to make sure I can read all the words so the kids will understand exactly what happened. I don't want them to have to ask me to unconfuse it."

Finally, it was time to share what they had been working on. Students who wanted to be called on had already written their names on the board so the teacher would know who was ready. During the next twenty-five minutes, Toni shared parts of her first draft for class feedback and responses, Jane shared a new lead sentence, and Pat read a completed section of Chapter Two in a piece he had been writing for over a week. At last, it was Stavros's turn. He proudly gathered up his story, walked to the front of the room, and proudly began to read: "The Lost Garage Door Opener, written and illustrated by Stavros and dedicated to my mom and dad."

When Stavros finished, he looked up proudly and said, "Any questions?" The class was ready for him. They knew they were expected to respond to all work with a positive statement first. They were also accustomed to asking clarifying questions, and they were comfortable expressing their opinions about a story or suggesting ideas for extending the writing. Comments for Stavros included: "I liked when you described all the places they looked for the garage door opener." "There were a lot of clues and I liked that you waited until the end of the story to find it." "Your friends helped you solve the mystery, just like *Frog and Toad* that we read." There were also questions, including "What gave you the idea for the story?" and "Did this really happen?"

Stavros handled the questions like a pro. The teacher offered a comment about how well the action fit together and made sense, something she had emphasized in a previous mini lesson. The principal (who had been invited by Stavros) said she was pleased that the story showed how everyone cooperated and worked together to solve the mystery, not getting angry or giving up.

When the sharing was over, Stavros donated his story to the class library, asking the teacher to make a copy of it so he could show it to his mom and then put it into his portfolio. The written reflection that he attached to the portfolio copy said, "I want to put this in my portfolio because it is the longest story I've written and my mom will be so proud of me. I made it like a real mystery with lots of clues and I worked hard on it." He also explained to the volunteer mom, who helped during Writers' Workshop, that he had a writer's corner set up in his room at home and was practicing writing all the time. He said that sometimes he liked to copy stories out of books, and other times, he liked to create his own stories. "Writers can do that, you know! They can write anything they want and make people laugh or cry."

Teacher Change over Time

Writers' Workshop in Bev Jones's class hadn't always gone this smoothly. In fact, when she moved to first grade from teaching kindergarten, Bev wasn't at all sure how or when to include writing in her curriculum. At the beginning of her first year teaching first grade, she believed that the students needed to know their letters and sounds before they could really learn to read or write. She knew they could "write" in their journals, since they had been doing that in kindergarten, often drawing their stories and dictating them to a teacher or mom to write under the pictures. She felt that to let them write on their own would be unbelievably difficult, for them and for her. How could anyone possibly manage 26 students who would all need help spelling words and getting their ideas onto paper?

During her annual goal setting, Bev told her principal that she planned to include writing at some point during the year. For now, however, she felt her students weren't ready to write, because they didn't know all the letters and sounds. The principal had just received a flier about a workshop Donald Graves was giving in the area, which indicated that children could write at the beginning of first grade. Would she be interested in going to see what she could learn? Bev agreed to go with another first grade teacher.

Graves spent the first half of the workshop talking about the writing process. He showed several examples of primary children choosing their own topics, drafting, and sharing their writing. He emphasized the importance of approximations and how children need to take risks in order to grow. Bev admitted to her colleague that after seeing these examples, she felt like she had underestimated her students. But how could she get this going? During lunch, the two tried to figure out how to include Writers' Workshop in an already crowded curriculum, how to organize the mini-lessons they were hearing about, and how to manage the writing experiences so that all the children could be actively involved.

The afternoon was filled with information about helping students choose topics they "care deeply" about, how to support them in their initial attempts, and the role of the teacher. At the end of the day, Bev bought books by Graves, Calkins, and Atwell and excitedly brought them back to school, determined to try to set up a Writers' Workshop in her classroom.

Back at school, Bev and her principal discussed and planned how to manage the time, the organization, and the whole Writers' Workshop process. The principal offered to come in on a regular basis to help with conferencing. She expressed an interest in learning more with Bev about writing process, in an attempt to understand how to make writing a more integral part of the overall curriculum in all the grades. With this kind of support and the interest of other teachers in her grade level, Bev followed Graves's suggestions for starting Writers' Workshop. Slowly, step by step, with his book in her hands, she moved into a new dimension of understanding how students learn about print and move into literacy.

One of Bev's first areas of discomfort was in giving up story starters. Beginnings like "Today I feel . . . ," "Yesterday I went . . . ," and "Pretend you are . . ." seemed to help students when they were stuck. On the other hand, Graves had pointed out the dangers of teaching children to depend on someone else to get them started. Bev reminded herself that if her long-term goal was to encourage independent, self-initiated writing, it made sense that her students must be involved in the entire writing process from beginning to end.

"Surviving Day One," part of Chapter One in Graves's *Writing: Teachers and Children at Work*, became Bev's road map for starting Writers' Workshop. She had given each child a writing folder with a blank sheet of paper inside the front cover, titled "Writing Ideas." Inside the back cover was another blank sheet, titled "What I Can Do as a Writer." The children had lined writing paper in front of them, and they waited to start writing.

Bev nervously stood in front of the chalkboard and began to talk about the ideas she had for writing her own personal story. She had read that the students had to begin to write about something they knew well—their life experiences were the richest source of writing ideas and the easiest to tap into. Demonstrating her thinking out loud, Bev wrote the name "Charlie" on the board, and told the children about her new puppy, Charlie: how she chose him, how she named him, and how she wished someone would invent a puppy toilet (the children howled). She then wrote down "My Vacation" and talked about how their car had a flat tire on the way to Wisconsin, and described the resort they stayed at, complete with swimming pool, miniature golf, and horses. Her last possible topic was about falling off her bike while riding with her friend. Bev asked the children which story they would like to hear more about. Charlie won, hands down. She drew a circle around it on the board.

Then she asked the students to think of their own stories. A few volunteers shared with the whole class. She asked everyone to team up and share with a partner. As they talked, she roamed the classroom, eavesdropping here and there and asking questions when she could see that something needed to be clarified or an important part might have been left out. After a few minutes of this partner sharing, the class discussed their ideas, noticing that there were a lot of topics about brothers, sisters, sports, trips, and pets.

Each child wrote down three ideas to write about, circled the one that was most interesting, and began to write. Bev remembered that Graves had said the teacher should write along with the children, and so she wrote as well. After five minutes of writing, Bev started to walk around the room again. Some children were busy writing their stories. Others were drawing pictures, and some were asking their neighbors how to spell words. A few said they were "thinking," and spent their time watching the other children write, hoping to get an idea.

Bev stopped next to Jimmy's desk. He wasn't writing. Bev knelt down beside him and said, "Tell me what you are thinking about writing. Just talk to me about it." Jimmy started to tell Bev about how he and his brother like to play "rough and tough" and that their mom always thought they were hurting each other. Bev told Jimmy to write just what he was saying, and started him out by repeating his story so he could hear the sounds in the words as she said them. "Me and My Brother" became one of Jimmy's first and best pieces.

Over time, and with gentle nudging from her principal/collaborator to try and take a risk, she began to trust the students to think of their own topics. Soon she was seeing stories about karate, vacations, pets, all kind of sports, "Fighting with my sister," and even "When my brother broke my arm." By the spring of the first year, the students rarely seemed to be at a loss for ideas, using their sharing time to generate new topics for their own writing. Their life experiences and outside interests took on much more importance as they learned that ideas for writing could be found in everything they were doing.

After this successful beginning, Bev began to read other professional material, discussing with other colleagues what worked, what was questionable, and what she hoped to do. As she moved more into the Writers' Workshop routine, she tried to manage her time so that writing could occur on a daily basis. Bev thought she could plan for drafting stories on Monday, conferencing on Tuesday, revising or rewriting on Wednesday, publishing on Thursday, and sharing and celebrating on Friday. This way, she could have Writers' Workshop every day throughout the week, and then spend the following week doing something else, returning to Writers' Workshop the week after.

While she was comfortable with this organization, her students didn't seem to be. They were not fitting into her management plan as smoothly as she had hoped. Some students were finishing their stories in a day, wanting to move on to a new topic right away. Others were writing chapters and wanted to continue their stories past the Friday deadline (even though she tried to hurry them up). These children often lost momentum and interest by the time Writers' Workshop came again two weeks later. Bev was most concerned about the quality of the stories some students were sharing. She felt there were too many short, colorless pieces with overly general statements—stories that seemed to have been given little thought by a writer in a rush to finish, share, and publish by Friday.

Once again, Bev and her principal talked. Their conversation made it clear that this was an example of management and structure impacting the children's learning in a negative way. While she was interested in helping children learn to control their own writing processes, the time frame she had set up was taking that control away! Bev decided to schedule Writers' Workshop for thirty minutes every other day for one month and to confer more closely with students as they chose their topics, trying to ensure that they were writing about things that excited them. Bev also realized she had done very little with helping the students respond to each other's writing. Going back through her workshop notes, she found an idea—she could put writing on a transparency so students could see it and ask questions about it. She thought about an experience that would be fun to write about and would appeal to her students. She decided to share a little secret with them.

The next morning, she gathered the children around, dimmed the lights, turned on the overhead projector, and read:

> At night when I'm tired and ready to go to bed, I turn down my soft blue blanket and slowly climb in. When my head hits the pillow, I relax and close my eyes. It feels so good after a long, busy day. But . . . before I go to sleep, I reach under my bed and feel around. There! A small box of candy waiting just for me. I take off the lid, choose one piece and pop it into my mouth!

She looked up at her students. They were staring at her, wide-eyed, mouths open. "Really?!" "Do you really do that every night?" "What kind of candy?" "Do you brush your teeth after?" "Did you do that when you were our age?"

Bev answered all their questions, and she added more information to her draft with a different color pen than the one she'd written the original story in. Then they talked about how their questions had made her rethink the story and how writers often change their stories to add interesting things that readers might want to know.

The next few weeks were spent emphasizing the idea that writers need good listeners and that listeners need to ask questions they really want to know the answers to. Writers were encouraged to carefully consider what their partners wanted to know, but to add or make changes only when it seemed right to them. Bev began to see a difference in their pieces.

Lifting the organizational constraints seemed to help enormously. With their newfound freedom, the students relaxed enough to experiment even more with other forms of writing, turning a story about a pet dog into a chapter book reminiscent of the *Henry and Mudge* series, or a sequel to *Danny and the Dinosaurs* with an accompanying fact book about dinosaurs. Personal writing was still going on, but Bev could see the reading/writing connection more clearly as the students tried their hands at mystery writing, memoirs, joke books, and predictable books.

Initially, as they were responding and asking questions of each other's writing, there was a total reluctance to add information or make changes. As Bev persisted in sharing her writing and demonstrating the impact of their questions on her pieces, they began to make changes in response to questions and comments. Bev could see this developing sense of audience in other ways—they were more comfortable rewriting their stories for "publishing" to make them as good as they could be. Knowing that others would read their writing became an incredible motivating factor to add information even *before* the questions were asked. Bev thought that anticipating readers' needs demonstrated a level of sophistication she would never have expected from first graders. More and more, her appreciation for their writing and thinking abilities grew.

"I Need Help!": Getting Parents into the Act

As the year proceeded, Bev felt that she alone couldn't meet the needs of all her students, who wanted help choosing topics, reading drafts, getting responses, editing, and publishing stories. Clearly, the students were learning to help and support each other, but she constantly wished she could clone herself three or four times! She remembered that when she visited another school, there were parent helpers working in a first-grade classroom on a scheduled basis during Writers' Workshop. But if she herself was just now gaining confidence with the writing process, how could she teach parents to do it? She thought about some of the key things she had learned that developing writers need, and after a long period of reflection, she decided it was what Ralph Fletcher talked about in *What a Writer Needs*: "Like a good music teacher, the writing teacher endures the bad melodies and shaky rhythms, stays patient, and picks out moments when the writing works well." That was it. If she could teach a few parents to be effective listeners (as she had already taught most of her students), and then teach them to see and comment on even one strength in a piece of writing, what a difference that could make to her students! Her students had become fairly skilled in asking genuine questions about each other's writing, but they all definitely needed to hear more about what was powerful in their work. Bev sent out a letter asking for parents who were interested in helping with Writers' Workshop to commit to three evenings to learn more about it. Ten parents showed up the first night.

Bev opened the first evening by asking the parents to talk about their own writing experiences in school. It seemed that everyone had a horror story to tell.

The parents' bad memories made them even more appreciative and supportive of Bev's goal of instilling a love of writing in her students.

She carefully explained the philosophy behind Writers' Workshop and used her "Bedtime Secret" piece to demonstrate topic selection, drafting, responding, and revising. They discussed invented spelling, why it's important for children to take risks with their writing, and how editing, the last phase of the writing process, helps writers learn about punctuation and standard spelling. It occurred to her that these parents needed their own positive writing experiences to carry into the workshop, even though there wasn't much planning time. She asked them to think of and share their own secrets. The sharing and laughing created such a warm feeling that when she asked them to write, the resistance was much lower than she had anticipated. Reading the short pieces aloud simply extended the bond they now felt.

Sessions two and three were spent looking at children's writing and learning to see the strengths. Bev used writing from her own classroom (with the authors' permission) and photocopied drafts from her growing collection of professional books on writing. The questions they explored focused primarily on, "How *could* you respond?" "What's one thing you could highlight for this writer?" Bev wanted them to explore alternative responses and try to get a sense of what might help. She and the parents ended the third night by developing a simple model to follow when they were volunteering for Writers' Workshop:

- Listen hard.
- Respond genuinely.
- Ask real questions.
- Encourage writers to talk more about their topics.
- Point out at least one strength.

They had also decided that it was important for the parents to see the same writers each time they came to the classroom so they could get to know the students' work and thinking well. Most parents were able to commit to meeting once a week for one hour. After the first few weeks, the *parents* requested another evening session to compare notes, get more ideas, and to ask questions. What Bev had originally conceived of as "Parent Training Sessions" had become a collaborative learning experience for all of them. She felt that the weight of needing to know everything about the writing process and Writers' Workshop had lifted. She, the students, and their parents continued to grow together.

In May of the first year of Writers' Workshop, she organized an "Authors' Tea." All parents were invited, and each student selected one piece of writing to share. Michael's piece seemed to exemplify the pride and confidence Bev's students felt in themselves:

I am Michael.

I am a writer.

I write about my favorite animals.

I write about spying.

I write about hiding.

I write about Superheroes.

I write about race cars.

I write about other states.
I write about buffalo.
I write at home.
I write on the bus.
I am Michael.
I am a writer.

Portfolios

Bev knew about portfolios when she started the workshop in her classroom but it was January before she felt she could give them any attention. In the meantime, the children had been saving almost all of their writing. By the end of the fall semester, everyone had at least three published pieces. When she did begin, she pulled out *Portfolio Portraits* and read Margaret Moss's article on portfolios in the first grade. She was relieved to see that Laurie Mansfield, the teacher in the article, had started with only five children.

Bev introduced the idea of portfolios using a family picture album: "Whenever I take a roll of film, my family and I look through all of the pictures and decide which ones we think are *really* special and why. Those are the ones that make it into the album." Each picture had a caption with a date, explaining what was happening and why it was memorable. Bev explained that this was the kind of "selecting and reflecting" she wanted them to do with their writing. "The pieces that you choose for your portfolios should be special to you in some way. I trust you to make your own choices. Occasionally, I might make a suggestion, but the final decision is yours. Sometimes it may not be clear to you exactly why a piece is special, so we can work on that together."

She asked if anyone had a piece they thought would be a candidate for their portfolio. Andrea suggested her "New Brother" piece. When Bev asked why, she said because her little brother is special to her. "So the topic is important and that's why you think the piece should go in?" Andrea agreed that that was exactly the reason. As children called out stories, poems, or nonfiction they had written, Bev began to help them with the reflective language they would need to talk about their writing and to understand their growth. Bev sent most of the class off to write and invited three children to stay and begin their portfolio selections with her. At the end of the workshop time, Bev asked all of the children to join her to talk about the first portfolio choices.

At first the reflections in Bev's classroom were "like it, love it, it's good, don't know" reflections. It made her nervous at first, because she began to wonder if children this age were capable of evaluating their work. Maybe she was asking too much. She remembered, though, that she had felt the same way about writing, and now look how far she had come! She resolved to hang in there.

She discovered that the children's reflections were often better when they could compare pieces. That way, they could see when they "first started to use periods," wrote "the longest piece I've ever written," put in "more action," and so forth. The reflections steadily improved, and Bev began to realize how invaluable her responses and the parent responses were in helping her students see more in their writing.

At the end of the year, Bev reflected on all she had learned about the writing process, Writers' Workshop, and first graders' capabilities—far beyond what she had ever imagined. She also asked her students to reflect on their learning over the year. Stavros wrote:

> I'm proud that I can ried and lorn and writ. I likt sharing my work with the othr kids. They liked my work and my stories. I writ at home all the tim. I teach my brodr how to ried and I ried my stories to him. My favrit thing I lornd was about spas and then animals. My mystry story was good to. Next year I want to lorn more and keep writing. I like to writ. It is how I get ideas out of my hed. Then I can ried them later and remembr them.

Reflective Commentary

In *The Art of Teaching Writing*, Calkins says, "Children can write sooner than we ever dreamed was possible." Like Bev, primary teachers around the country are becoming aware of young children's composing abilities. Like Bev, many primary grade teachers are learning about the writing process so they can support these natural talents. The writing process and writing workshops have become initial transition points for many teachers interested in curricular change. Writing process can be a wonderful place to start rethinking teaching/learning perspectives because it doesn't usually conflict with an existing program. In fact, in our profession, we are still coming to terms with the absolute need for a daily commitment to writing. There is irony in the fact that our schools, the very institutions that are supposed to nurture literacy, still give precious little time for extended, uninterrupted writing every day. One of our main challenges as teachers considering language arts standards is to find ways to devote more time to actual writing. A skill as complex as writing can never develop fully with only brief, occasional liaisons.

Besides time, other issues are critical for developing writers. We have all witnessed classroom scenes that make us reflect on the philosophical goodness of our curricular messages—a first-grade student carefully and laboriously spending all of her writing time placing an index finger between each word so the spacing is perfect, a seven-year-old blocked so completely that he will only write those words he can spell "exactly right." Perfect spaces and spelling that distract from the importance of ideas will not help children love to write. Through the eye-opening research of people like Donald Graves, Lucy Calkins, Donald Murray, and Nancie Atwell, we have learned that, above all, writers need purpose and audience, as well as what Calkins calls "real human reasons to write."

Many teachers introduce the writing process as Bev did—by demonstrating and encouraging personal narratives, showing children how to tap into the rich experiences that fill *all* of their lives. Graves reminds us that many children come to school believing that there is no significance in their lives. If these children are fortunate enough to have teachers who recognize, value, and help them tap the stories they carry inside, they have a great chance of becoming learners who think through writing and people who see themselves as writers.

In the past, writing in school has been viewed as so hard and distasteful that our children needed to be enticed and motivated with things like "story starters." Calkins points out that "there is a world of difference between 'motivating writing' and helping people become deeply and personally involved in their own writing" (p. 12). Teachers must begin writing in their classrooms by assuming not only that children *can* write, but that their lives are filled with events worth holding on to, worth sharing with someone else, and above all, worth thinking about and exploring through written language. Beginning writers must feel the power that comes from discovering meaning as they write their personal stories; they must feel the satisfaction that comes from an appreciative audience laughing, applauding, and often writing back.

While beginning with personal experience stories is a solid move into the writing process, teachers who immerse their students in literature and nonfiction find that children soon want to try various forms of expression. Children bring their lives and interests with them into the classroom, and those are immediately available as topics for writing, but their lives and interests expand with every read-aloud or independent reading time and sharing of pieces written in the classroom. Topics, genre, and formats are all contagious, but only when children hear and see and examine each others' writing. When Carl desperately wanted to create a pop-up book to display the information on insects he had been studying, suddenly four other kindergartners were clamoring to learn the procedure. When Janelle wrote a travel brochure after her trip to Yellowstone, the second-grade classroom was flooded with travel information that included maps, travel guides, hotels, and "Things that Children Would Love to Do on Vacation."

Classrooms fill with groundswells like these when children's pieces have voice and when strong voices have an audience. In Kathy Egawa's multi-age classroom, she says there are many ways to encourage children to write, but tapping that "real energy" in beginning writers depends on the audience. What kinds of audiences transform children into passionate writers? For some children, dialoguing with the teacher in a daily journal proves effective. For others it is the anticipation of a pen-pal letter. For one classroom, it was regular e-mail exchanges with parents—this was a way to encourage busy moms and dads to slow down and talk with their children. Most young children are not accustomed to providing their own motivation, and most five- and six-year-olds are not conscious of what conditions turn them into eager participants. Teachers have to know that, and they have to work hard to discover that. All children have to be introduced to writing in supportive ways.

Kathleen Visovatti introduces writing to her students by asking them to draw self-portraits and then write their first impressions of school. She reassures them that any kind of writing or pretend writing is fine, and when the inevitable questions come about spelling, she gives them a few strategies to rely on, such as, "Just write down the first sound that you hear and then draw a line for the rest." After that, if they ask, she points to the strategies posted on the wall and tells

them that she can't help them because spelling is part of the job of writing. Anyway, she tells them, spelling their own way shows her that they are thinking, testing out ideas like scientists do. It becomes clear to them that she values approximation and risk-taking. Kathleen knows these practices are essential to growth. She is absolutely firm about the no-helping rule and says she never breaks it. However, she also says, "I reassure them emphatically—promise,

promise, promise—that if I can't read something, I'll be sure to come and ask them. But I also tell them that the things that will be made available for public reading, like the first impressions pieces and published stories, *do* need to be spelled correctly and that I will help them when they get to that point."

Some teachers are reluctant to encourage invented spelling because they still feel unsure that their students will progress into standard form. Sulzby puts those fears to rest in the April 1992 issue of *Language Arts*, where she summarizes all that we know about children's emergent writing and their transitioning into conventional writing. "When given a supportive context, be it home or school, young children compose connected written discourse using emergent forms long before they hold conventional ideas about writing. . . . They move from emergent forms and understandings to become conventional writers with conventional concepts about writing. . . . Writing development from emergent to conventional understandings has been documented in the United States across sociocultural groups and in many other countries using different writing systems and languages" (p. 291).

Calkins (1986) suggests that students who are having trouble spelling are simply not doing enough writing. A lack of emphasis on standard spelling while writers are carving out their ideas doesn't mean that spelling isn't taken into consideration later (or during the writing process itself), and it certainly doesn't mean that students will get sloppy or develop bad habits. Spelling is an attractive area for teachers to engage in their own informal research. Even tracking one child's spelling of a few words over time can be enormously illuminating. Consider Amie's move from invented to standard spelling of "Bloomington" as she wrote letters to her aunt over many months:

blueeit
bluemingtn
blomingtion
Bloomington

In Kathleen's classroom, Writers' Workshop includes choices: journals, letters, birthday cards, stories, and information books developed from topics they are researching. She tracks each child's writing to make sure that, at least some of the time, everyone is doing extended writing, such as stories or information books. She is careful to highlight spelling and other writing strategies during the whole-group shares at the end of each writing workshop.

First-grade teacher Pat Riordan says the most wonderful part of writing is the sense her children have of being authors; the reading/writing connection is strong in her classroom. "After a few weeks of immersing them in beautiful picture books and great read-alouds, and giving them time to write themselves, I notice that they start turning to literature to look more closely at decisions, an author's style, where ideas come from—right down to the dedications in the backs of the books which they start doing in their own writing. Recently, I have started reading nonfiction books aloud on a regular basis, so now they spontaneously study these books, too, to see how they're organized and how the ideas are developed. Their books are valued as much as the commercial ones. It's so evident when they check each other's books out to take home more than the published trade ones."

Pat also confides, "I always regret that when I was six years old, I wasn't coming home with those beautiful artifacts. Twenty years from now these children will wonder what they were thinking and doing and were interested in when they were five and six and seven years old. And then they'll pull out the books they wrote, and they'll know."

A Thinking Process, Not a Linear Procedure

Understanding writing as a process is one of the first struggles that Bev went through in her attempts to set up a Writers' Workshop. When teachers think about the primary elements involved in writing—topic selection, rehearsal, drafting, revision, and editing—it is easy to fall into the trap of believing that it is a step-by-step, linear procedure. Bev began by doing what seemed logical to her: assigning the "first step" in writing, topic selection, to the first day the children were supposed to write, and proceeding from there. However, processes do not unfold in neat, clean, definitive boxes.

When Katelin, a first grader, decided to write about her hamster, it was a decision filled with general images and an intent to show how much she loved her pet. During three writing workshops she drew and redrew; she started one sentence and then another; she talked to different friends about convincing her parents to buy the hamster, her responsibility to take care of it, and how last weekend she discovered there was no water in the cage. That was the starting point of her writing, and the real topic of her story became "Learning to Be Responsible." She had to discover it through conversation, trying out an idea here and there and drawing her meanings. In contrast, Patrick, sitting next to her, zeroed in on his "Facts about Trains" booklet and in three workshops had the entire text written, illustrated, and shared. Katelin's efforts to begin drafting her story simultaneously put her in a position to rethink her topic. Katelin shows us that writing is not a step-by-step, predictable procedure. Rather, it is a complex process filled with recursion and strategies that encourage meaning-making. The writing process unfolds differently for different writers, depending on purpose, experience, and the writing context itself. Bissex (1980) says that "the logic by which we teach is not always the logic by which children learn." Curricular structures must follow, not precede, what is known about learning processes. When Bev opened the structure of her Writers' Workshop to accommodate individual movement and experimentation, she helped support the learning efforts of all her students.

Portfolios

Even though the concept of portfolios has entered our educational consciousness, there are still many questions about them. Key issues tend to center around ownership, management, and learning potential.

Portfolios belong to the learner. That doesn't mean that they don't have tremendous power to help teachers observe and evaluate young writers, their thinking, their strategies, their struggles; but, primarily, they are personal learner stories. Jane Hansen is fond of saying that portfolios should show who a learner is and who she wants to be. Students are ultimately responsible for selecting what goes into a portfolio and for saying why it's an important part of their story; no one else can make that kind of judgment about significance.

One of the concerns about portfolio development is that the implementation too often remains at a collection level, more akin to a clerical task than an integral part of a learning cycle. Tierney, Carter, and Desai (1991) note that "portfolios are not merely storage areas for student work. Instead, students are involved in self-assessment as they organize their portfolios, select and arrange their materials, reflect upon what they have achieved, plan their future work, share their work with others, and offer introductory critiques to accompany their work" (p. 108). Portfolios should provide golden opportunities for students to select and reflect upon significant events throughout any school year. Portfolios are becoming an indispensable part of curriculum because they are teaching us valuable lessons about authentic assessment. They help create a more complete picture of students' developing literacy/learning abilities than any paper-and-pencil test ever could. With portfolios, students have a chance to look at themselves from many different angles.

Roxanne Henkin says that one of the deepest impacts portfolios have had on education is to teach us that our classrooms need deeper reflection. A portfolio's greatest value is that it gives each student a chance to take a reflective

stance on learning and, in the process, learn even more (Crafton, 1994). Reflection is a critical aspect of all effective learning. Portfolios are intimately tied to our understandings of learning and literacy. They can become an opportunity for students to stand back and become involved in the evaluative dimension of their learning process. Learning to reflect, however, takes time. Classrooms have to operate on the understanding that psychological distance is a key dimension of effective learning. When we look at the world around us and consider the range of productive work in which people engage every day, there is no evidence of formalized testing as a measure of success. But there is plenty of evidence of disciplined reflection. The world is filled with examples of self-evaluation that help guide, support, and refine the pursuit of worthwhile goals. Artists collect photographs of their work to show the range of their skill; musicians keep journals to help them remember the nuances of successful performances; master actors keep reflective notes about the relationship between intentional dramatic variations and audience response. In an effort to encourage reflection as an integral part of learning, classroom evaluation should resemble the kinds of intimate monitoring that skilled learners use outside of the classroom. Graves emphasizes that this kind of reflection has to be ongoing and that assembling a portfolio cannot come too quickly. He teaches us that students must constantly shuffle and evaluate their work throughout the year. "This is slow work for both teacher and student" (1992, p. 3). But it's hard to imagine that self-knowledge could come without steady effort.

Portfolios often join a context of curriculum reform in progress. One of the most exciting discoveries about the potential of portfolios to inform learning and the learner is that individual standards are often higher, broader, and deeper than those imposed on the outside. Rief (1990) has highlighted the notion of "internal criteria" to remind us that one of our major responsibilities as educators is to help children learn to critically judge their own work.

What Key Standards Emerge and Interact in This Context?

Students read a range of print and nonprint texts. Students read and responded to each other's stories. They studied and created visual texts like story illustrations and travel brochures.

Students apply a range of strategies. Writers responded to each other's writing in a variety of ways including stating opinions and asking questions for clarification. While composing their stories, they experienced a range of strategies such as rereading, adding details or new information, and illustrating their texts. Students explored different strategies as they wrote for different audiences and purposes—stories written for peers and the teacher, pieces published for out-of-classroom circulation from the class library, texts revised for presentation at the "Author's Tea."

Students adapt conventions to communicate effectively. Students varied their strategies in writing. Depending on audience and purpose, they used different organizational formats, selected different language, varied the level of formality, and included visual information like illustrations and diagrams to help clarify their print messages. Their writing included primarily personal stories, but also informational books on sports, dinosaurs, caring for pets, and simple chapter-books and adventure stories.

Students research issues and interests. As students began to write non-fiction, some identified specific topics to research (dinosaurs, caring for pets, whales and sharks, etc.). While books were the dominant resource, some interviewed classmates, siblings, parents, and teacher to help them gather a wider range of information. The findings of these individual and sometimes collaborative projects were often shared through a published book.

Students use knowledge of language structure, language conventions, media techniques, and genre. While reading fairy tales, students discussed the structure of that genre and later compared how fairy tales are organized differently than mysteries, adventures, and predictable books.

Students participate in a variety of literacy communities. Every student in Bev's classroom belonged to the writers' community within their classroom. Within this group, they evaluated ideas for writing, listened and responded to each other's writing-in-progress, helped one another apply conventions appropriately, noted what they liked and disliked in each other's writing, and reflected on writing strategies that worked and didn't work for them. Beyond that, each student belonged to flexible peer-response groups in which they read and responded to one another's writing throughout the year. In preparation for the "Author's Tea," students read and critiqued one another's read-aloud performance. Students also asked one another to help select "Best Writing" for their portfolios.

Students use spoken, written, and visual language to accomplish their own purposes. Some parents told Bev that their children were keeping notebooks at home so they could record topics they wanted to write about and draft stories, letters, lists, and drawings.

References and Other Resources

Applebee, A. (1978). *The child's concept of story.* Chicago: University of Chicago Press.

Atwell, N. (1987). *In the middle: Writing, reading, and learning with adolescents.* Portsmouth, NH: Heinemann.

Bissex, G. (1980). *GNYS AT WRK: A child learns to write and read.* Cambridge, MA: Harvard University Press.

Butler, A., & Turbill, J. (1984). *Towards a reading-writing classroom.* Portsmouth, NH: Heinemann.

Calkins, L. M. (1983). *Lessons from a child: On the teaching and learning of writing.* Portsmouth, NH: Heinemann.

Calkins, L. M. (1986). *The art of teaching writing.* Portsmouth, NH: Heinemann.

Clay, M. (1976). *What did I write?* London: Heinemann.

Crafton, L. K. (1991). *Whole language: Getting started . . . moving forward.* Katonah, NY: Richard C. Owen.

Crafton, L. K. (1994). *Challenges of holistic teaching: Answering the tough questions.* Norwood, MA: Christopher-Gordon.

Dyson, A. H. (1989). *The multiple worlds of child writers: Friends learning to write.* New York: Teachers College Press.

Goodman, K. (1986). *What's whole in whole language?* Portsmouth, NH: Heinemann.

Graves, D. H. (1978). *Balance the basics: Let them write.* New York: Ford Foundation.

Graves, D. H. (1983). *Writing: Teachers and children at work.* Portsmouth, NH: Heinemann.

Graves, D., & Sunstein, B. (Eds.). (1992). *Portfolio portraits.* Portsmouth, NH: Heinemann.

Harste, J. C., Short, K. G., & Burke, C. (1988). *Creating classrooms for authors.* Portsmouth, NH: Heinemann.

Harste, J. C., Woodward, V. A., & Burke, C. (1984). *Language stories and literacy lessons.* Portsmouth, NH: Heinemann.

Murray, D. M. (1985). *A writer teaches writing* (2nd ed). Boston: Houghton Mifflin.

Newman, J. M. (1984). *The craft of children's writing.* Ontario: Scholastic.

Newman, J. M. (Ed.). (1985). *Whole language: Theory in use.* Portsmouth, NH: Heinemann.

Rief, L. (1991). *Seeking diversity: Language arts with adolescents.* Portsmouth, NH: Heinemann.

Short, K. G., & Pierce, K. M. (Eds.). (1990). *Talking about books.* Portsmouth, NH: Heinemann.

Smith, F. (1978). *Reading without nonsense.* New York: Teachers College Press.

Smith, F. (1982). *Writing and the writer.* Portsmouth, NH: Heinemann.

Sulzby, E. (1992). Transitions from emergent to conventional writing. *Language Arts, 69,* 290–297.

Tierney, R., Carter, M. A., & Desai, L. E. (1991). *Portfolio assessment in the reading-writing classroom.* Norwood, MA: Christopher-Gordon.

Trelease, J. (1985). *The read-aloud handbook* (Rev. Ed.). New York: Penguin.

Watson, D. J., Burke, C., & Harste, J. (1989). *Whole language: Inquiring voices.* Ontario: Scholastic.

Wilde, S. (1992). *You kan red this! Spelling and punctuation for whole language classrooms, K–6.* Portsmouth, NH: Heinemann.

CHAPTER THREE

REAL-WORLD LEARNING AND EMERGENT LITERACY

Before reading, consider . . .
- *What strategies you use as a reader.*
- *What you have observed about young children interacting with print in non-school settings (e.g., home, grocery store, car, museums).*
- *What you know about emergent literacy.*

Pat Riordan had been teaching first grade at an inner-city elementary school for many years. The student population consisted of children from multiethnic, multilingual backgrounds. Using a basal reading series was a struggle for both teacher and students. Pat noticed the children's frustrations with the contrived language of the basal material, and began to take graduate classes on reading in hope of resolving some of the struggles.

Sue Smeaton joined the staff at the same inner-city school immediately after completing her undergraduate studies. She had a strong interest in setting up a child-centered kindergarten curriculum. Initially, she implemented a "Letter of the Week" approach. While this approach moved away from worksheets and skill-and-drill curriculum, Sue continued to question the kindergarten program's focus. She was now centering everything around the letters, not around the learners in her classroom—which was exactly what she wanted to change.

Sue and Pat, after discovering each other's interests, began a series of in-person and written conversations about how to change their teaching. As they talked and got to know each other, they discovered that they both believed learning could (and should) occur in contexts that are natural and purposeful—from a *child's* perspective. Exactly what did that mean? And how could they structure their classrooms to reflect that belief? How could they create kindergarten and first-grade curricula that engaged children in real-world learning, reading, writing, speaking, and listening?

Along with their reflective conversations, journal articles and professional books helped Pat and Sue explore their primary concern about authentic learning and language arts. They slowly began to make changes.

Natural Opportunities for Reading, Writing, and Talking

September 10

Dear Sue,

Kate brought a caterpillar to school today. She found it while visiting her grandmother. Grandma had carefully placed it in a jar with sticks and leaves. It has already started to form a chrysalis. The kids were so excited! I was surprised that this small piece of nature inspired so much talk and so many genuine questions. Their enthusiasm makes me want to pursue this interest in the classroom. I'm not sure where to go from here.

Pat

September 14

Dear Pat,

What an opportunity! Have you ever read Eric Carle's book *The Very Hungry Caterpillar?* How about setting up a nature study with your class? Think about what kids do when they find these things in their backyards. Maybe you could put a notebook by the nature center and they could write or draw their observations there! Carle's book would help you get more literature into the classroom, and along with the nature center, it would help them begin to answer their questions.

I introduced a sign-in sheet and journals to the kindergartners. Each morning when they arrive, they sign their names in whatever way they can, and then have time to journal. I have even initiated dialogue journals with some of the kids. I've noticed that the kindergartners are becoming more comfortable with sharing their entries. How is journaling going in first grade? Also, let me know what you decide to do with the caterpillar.

Sue

September 22

Sue,

It's amazing to me how this caterpillar has become the center of our curriculum. So much learning has come naturally from the students' questions. The kids' journals are filling up with drawings of the chrysalis, and they have begun writing their observations. After reading *The Very Hungry Caterpillar*, many of the kids created their own mini-books, borrowing the pattern from Eric Carle. How is the writing going in kindergarten?

Pat

September 25

Dear Pat,

Having 28 five-year-olds in the class has been a real challenge. It's amazing how the kids have connected with each other, given the fact that some of them don't speak the same language. I wish I could magically become multilingual (even bilingual!). But it seems we are still steadily becoming a community.

Right now, I'm struggling to follow the kids' leads. Today, while talking on the phone in the dramatic play area, Mark decided that we needed a class phone book. He went about collecting the information he needed, and began to compile it into a phone book! I began to notice my kids exchanging phone numbers and writing phone messages. It felt right giving up some of the activities I had planned for the day so that the kids could continue with this project, but what about the things we need to cover? What do you think?

Sue

September 27

Dear Sue,

I really like that phone book idea. The fact that it came from the kids makes it more meaningful. Their keen interest provided powerful motivation. Thinking about that experience makes me wonder how I can create opportunities like that for my class. Any ideas?

I wasn't sure what you meant about "covering" things—content or skills or what? I'm learning in one of my graduate classes about how to make close observation of skills and strategies *as the children are using them* during meaningful experiences. I can share that with you.

Pat

September 30

Pat,

You wouldn't believe how the kids took over that phone book project. They decided to publish the final draft on the computer. The typing took them several days, but the kids were determined to finish the book on their own. All of this made me realize that learning really can occur in situations that mirror the real world. I'm thinking about setting up a "restaurant" in one of the centers. There would be so many opportunities for real reading and writing. In an article I read, Burke suggested setting up a message board in the classroom. Why don't you try that with your first graders? Keep me "posted"!

Sue

October 3

Sue,

Thanks for the great idea! The message board turned out to be a simple way to get some real writing going in my classroom. I wrote each child a message and quickly got responses. I'm also using the message board to post newspaper clippings about special events that might be of interest to the kids. I've been encouraging their families to write messages at home as well. Messages are even appearing in their lunch boxes! Look at the one

To Mom: I Love You. Thank You for the good lunch. Give me a big hug when you get home.

that Kate wrote back to her Mom! The kids are getting more of a sense that print conveys meaning. You might want to think about trying this in your classroom as well. Have a great afternoon!

Pat

P.S.: Remember when we talked about making observations during real reading and writing experiences? Well, notice how Kate is experimenting with periods in her note to her Mom. I want to ask her about it so I can understand her thinking better. I made a Xerox of her note and put it in her folder—now I can watch to see how this develops for her.

Through conversation and journaling, Sue and Pat began to realize that these seemingly insignificant oral and written language events made powerful contributions to the development of the child as a learner. They wondered how they could restructure their classrooms to make these events more likely to occur. Initially, they looked for ways to create a print-rich environment and encourage purposeful talk, providing children with more authentic opportunities for reading, writing, and speaking.

Sue noticed that the kindergartners had taken an interest in menus from neighborhood restaurants. They were beginning to "play restaurant," assigning roles as servers, cooks, and customers. This seemed like a natural opportunity to expand upon the children's interest. Remembering that one student, Quoviet, had parents who owned a local Thai restaurant, Sue invited the children to ask Quoviet questions about his experiences. During this exchange, the idea was suggested that Quoviet's parents visit the classroom to share their experiences as restaurant owners. The children were excited when Quoviet's parents invited them to visit their restaurant. This outing sparked interest in setting up a restaurant in the kindergarten class. Over several days, one section of the classroom was transformed into the "Kid Cafe." The group collected pots and pans, created their own menus, and designed place mats, customer checks, and a reservation book. Uniforms added the final touch. Children created cook hats and aprons. The customers enjoyed using the "dress-up" clothes for "a night on the town." A cash register gave the children the opportunity to experiment with money. Sue noticed that the sound of

Purposeful writing: students create a poster to help find a classmate's shoes.

restaurant "talk" began to permeate the classroom. Children could be heard asking, "Smoking or non-smoking?" "How many in your party?" and "Are you ready to order?" Much of the language, which the children had internalized over time from their own restaurant experiences, began to spill out into the classroom restaurant. After reading Tomie de Paola's *Strega Nona,* the group made home-made egg-noodle pasta to be served at the "Kid Cafe." The children measured ingredients, worked the pasta maker, and prepared for the "feast." Parent volunteers staffed the kitchen, helping small groups cook the pasta and prepare the sauce. Invitations written by the children asked office personnel to join the kindergartners for lunch at the "Kid Cafe." Each child had the opportunity to cook in the kitchen and serve someone in the "restaurant." During a large group discussion, the children commented on their own favorite home-cooked dinners. As a group, the class decided to create a class cookbook, bringing in home recipes to share. Each family contributed a favorite to the first edition of the "Kid Cafe Cookbook."

In an effort to convince her first graders that they could already read, and to bring more real-world experiences into the classroom, Pat began to explore the topic of environmental print. She brought in cereal and toothpaste packages, which she knew the children would be able to read easily. She then invited her students to search their cabinets at home for packages they could read. Together the class created a bulletin board displaying these artifacts. She encouraged all the little stories connected to these items: "I was amazed at just how much these kids had to say about their favorite cereals and brushing their teeth!" Neighborhood walks provided another opportunity for the first graders to examine print in their environment. While walking with their fourth-grade "buddies," the children drew some of these signs in notebooks and talked about their meaning. The familiarity of so many of the signs—traffic signs, business signs, and store logos—helped boost the children's confidence in themselves as readers. On another outing, the children took pictures of some of their favorite signs. Tana Hoban's book *Signs* provided further opportunities to explore this topic. As a final project, the children created their own picture book of environmental print from the photographs taken on their walk.

As primary teachers, both Pat and Sue were aware of the need for young children to talk freely. They noticed the amount of conversation that surrounded the caterpillar study, the environmental print focus, and the Kid Cafe. They were excited about the "natural integration" that had occurred with these experiences, but they felt that they should also rethink the oral language opportunities in their classrooms from a real-world perspective in the same way they were rethinking reading and writing. Both classrooms had a sharing time each morning where volunteers could talk about anything they wanted to. Pat and Sue agreed that they would watch the children for a few days during this time and then talk freely themselves as well.

"If you seen two black shoes, bring it to [room] 10. Leo's Black Shoes."

October 10

Dear Sue,

The environmental print theme was a hit! Several parents have mentioned that their kids are driving them crazy reading everything in sight.

The children's parents, as well as myself, have begun to realize that neighborhood signs and other print in the world provide natural opportunities for learning to read. It's great to feel so good about what's happening in your classroom!

I've already noticed some things about sharing time. Sometimes I think my responses are not as great as they should be. I'm wondering if I'm responding to what is important to the child who is sharing (you know how they can have ten topics going at a time!). Have you noticed this?

Pat

October 11

Dear Pat,

I know exactly what you mean about responding to the stories! I always respond positively, but because there are so many kids in the classroom, I don't ask many questions or get clarification when I need it. I definitely feel like I want to have fewer children sharing each day so we can stress the value of what they are trying to say more. I'm going to work harder at hearing what is important in their stories from their perspective.

While these real-world experiences have added a new dimension to the classroom, I am unsure of where to go from here. Looking for ways to make classroom experiences more meaningful is definitely a good place to start, but what about the parents' concerns about their children being "ready to read"? (It seems like such a strange question when their children are already reading so many things!) Also, the lack of worksheets coming home makes them wonder if their children are learning. Communication with parents will be important as we continue to restructure our classrooms. I think having parents involved in the "Kid Cafe" was a valuable opportunity for them to see the learning in action, but I also need to consider those parents who have tight work schedules. The questions keep coming.

Sue

October 13

Dear Sue,

I think you have to remember to trust your instincts about how your children are learning. I have begun to look at how kids learn to read in a different way. You know that I have been questioning the use of the basal material with beginning readers. All of those workbook pages, skill packets, vocabulary builders, and skills tests! I rarely have time for the enrichment activities that look more interesting and meaningful for the kids. Well, last night in my graduate class, Linda Crafton read *Brown Bear, Brown Bear, What Do You See?* by Bill Martin, Jr. She identified it as a predictable book. Linda talked about the ways these books support beginning readers. The text has a predictable pattern and natural language, as opposed to the contrived text and controlled language of the basal material. Linda also shared a book list with us. I plan to introduce some of these books to my first graders, and I am anxious to see how they respond.

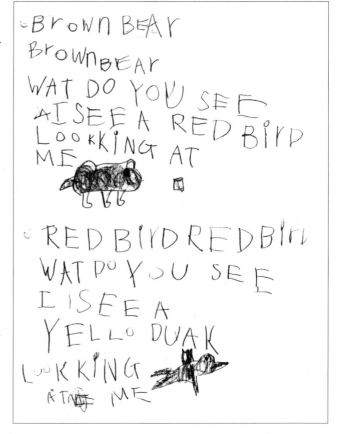

I like your idea of slowing down Sharing Time (we are now calling it Talking Time!). I think I'm getting better at seeing the world through six-year-old eyes—I feel more and more that what is important to them has to become important to me and my teaching (do you think that *has* to include Ninja Turtles?!). I'm considering dividing Talking Time into small groups, after we spend a few weeks reflecting on how to respond to and ask questions about what is important to the speaker. Do you think that would work in kindergarten?

Pat

October 15

Dear Pat,

It was exciting to hear about your discovery! I heard quite a lot about Bill Martin, Jr. in my children's literature class in college. We examined a series of books which he wrote as an alternative to basal material. I'm anxious to see the list that Linda shared. Your comments about predictable books made me think about how my kindergartners respond with such enthusiasm to nursery rhymes, songs and poetry (Do you know *Anna Banana: One Hundred Jump Rope Rhymes?)* Now I'm writing most of them on chart paper—the kids have a choice to read them with a partner during Reading Workshop, and they love it! I have to think some more about how to restructure Sharing Time.

Thanks! Sue

October 17

Sue,

I have introduced several predictable books, and I am excited to see how quickly they are becoming class favorites. At the end of each day, the kids are eager to take books home to show family members how they can read. The children's confidence in themselves as readers has grown due to the successful experience with these books. How is it working for you?

Pat

October 19

Pat,

Things are great! I see the same confidence developing in the kindergartners. "Reading readiness" has taken on new meaning for me. The enthusiasm and connectedness these children have with books support their very early attempts to read. Parents are also commenting on the excitement and interest they see at home. At the end of the day, each child chooses a book to take home to read. They each have a plastic "ziplock" bag to carry the book to and from school. The kids sign out the books themselves! Boy, did that take some time to fine tune, but now the kids have the whole system going. Each morning they hang their plastic bags on hooks which hang under their names. The class "librarian" makes a quick check-in. An empty hook means a book hasn't been returned.

It's exciting—I have even noticed that their language is flourishing. While I was greeting the children this morning in the rain, Adela quoted from a poem we recently read, "It's a misty, moisty morning, Mrs. Smeaton!"

Have a restful weekend, Sue

Toward a Literature-Based Reading Program

Pat and Sue continued their journaling, brought more and more predictable books into the classroom, and expanded Sharing Time so the children had more time to talk about topics that interested them. They watched closely as the predictable patterns and meaningful language supported their multilingual students, not only as readers, but as language users. They also observed their young students easing themselves into literacy, comfortably picking up a book and "talking like a book," as Marie Clay suggests. Big books and predictable books provided natural opportunities for children to develop an awareness of print and build sight vocabulary, as well as building prediction and comprehension strategies. In addition, the predictable pattern became a springboard for students to author their own books.

Pat and Sue's exploration into the use of predictable books led to a dialogue with their administrator, Tom Eber, about replacing the basals and workbooks with predictable material and trade books. They invited Tom into their classrooms to observe readers in action. In addition, they encouraged him to take home some of the material to read with his own young children. Impressed by what he observed at home and in their classrooms, Tom's own transition began. With his administrative support, the school slowly began to move toward a literature-based reading program. As they began to expand the use of literature in the classroom, Pat and Sue faced several major issues.

Initially, money was the biggest concern. They wanted to make a change, but they needed funds, and the school had a limited budget. In the beginning, many teachers purchased books on their own. Then, the administration made a commitment by investing in high-quality literature rather than textbooks and workbooks for reading. Bonus points from book club orders provided classrooms with "free" books. Circulation at the local public library skyrocketed as children obtained library cards and teachers made weekly trips to supplement the classroom and school libraries. Teachers shared books and ideas on how to use literature in the classrooms. Staff members attended workshops and read professional books and periodicals.

There were also grim realities. Some teachers were more comfortable with the basal material and workbooks. Parents needed to be reassured. Teachers needed ongoing encouragement and support as they examined ways to implement literature in the classroom. Communication was critical at this juncture.

> November 1
>
> Dear Pat,
>
> I think that our unit meetings have been such a help. Your suggestion to share literature at each session is super! And our brainstorming sessions on the strengths of different books are helpful. I am anxious to read *Going on a Bear Hunt* to the kindergartners. It'll be interesting to hear their responses to the story—the alliteration in that book is wonderful. I'm glad that Kathy shared that book with us. What's new in first grade?
>
> Sue

Pat and Sue's Favorite Predictable Books

Asch, F. (1982). *Happy Birthday Moon*. New York: Scholastic.

Bonn, R. (1961). *I Know An Old Lady*. New York: Scholastic.

Brown, M. W. (1942). *The Runaway Bunny*. New York: Harper & Row.

Carle, E. (1977). *The Grouchy Ladybug*. New York: Crowell.

Carle, E. (1984). *The Very Busy Spider*. New York: Philomel.

Carle, E. (1979). *The Very Hungry Caterpillar*. New York: Collins.

Cowley, J. (1986). *Greedy Cat*. New York: Richard C. Owen.

Flack, M. (1932). *Ask Mr. Bear*. New York: Macmillan.

Galdone, M. (1932). *The Gingerbread Boy*. New York: Seabury.

Goss, J. L., & Harste, J. (1981). *It Didn't Frighten Me*. School Book Fairs.

Guarino, D. (1989). *Is Your Mama a Llama?* New York: Scholastic.

Martin, B. Jr. (1983). *Brown Bear, Brown Bear, What Do You See?* New York: Holt, Rinehart & Winston.

Neitzel, S. (1989). *The Jacket I Wear in the Snow*. New York: Greenwillow.

Shaw, C. (1947). *It Looked Like Spilt Milk*. New York: Harper & Row.

Wood, A. (1983). *The Napping House*. San Diego, CA: Harcourt Brace Jovanovich.

Zemach, M. (1965). *The Teeny, Tiny Woman*. New York: Scholastic.

November 4

Dear Sue,

It was helpful for me to hear how teachers are using various types of literature to develop strategies for reading and writing. Every book seems to lend itself to something. Today we read different versions of *The Three Little Pigs.* As a group we discussed similarities and differences in these tales. We followed up with a Readers' Theater. I am amazed at how a

Readers' Theater

Readers' Theater focuses on bringing stories and characters alive through oral interpretation. Unlike plays, there is little or no costuming or movement, no stage sets, and no memorized lines. The focus in Readers' Theater is therefore on the literature, not on the actors, and on the readers communicating with the audience through the literature. Literature becomes a living experience for both the readers and the audience through the use of facial expressions, voice, and a few gestures. As groups try several different readings of the same story, these readings highlight multiple interpretations of texts. Readers are helped to see that reading is an active and open process of constructing meaning.

Procedure

1. Multiple copies of literature or scripts are needed. The literature chosen for Readers' Theater should have a great deal of dialogue, interesting characters, rich and rhythmic language, and a storyline with suspense or conflict and an element of humor or surprise. Folktales are especially good sources.

2. The literature can be adapted to make a Readers' Theater script. The adaptations can include omitting extraneous parts, shortening long speeches or descriptive sections, and using a narrator to make connections between scenes. Most adaptations can be done with only minimal rewriting.

3. Copies of the literature should be available for each reading part. Each reader should use a highlighter to indicate the parts to be read on his/her copy.

4. Readers may decide to stand or sit and decide how they will position themselves in relation to one another.

5. A practice session with a small group as the audience may generate suggestions for revision.

6. Students present the Readers' Theater. During a performance, readers sit or stand facing the audience and read their parts from the scripts, using their vocal expressions to bring life to the story.

7. Teachers should encourage both informal and formal presentations of Readers' Theater.

8. Readers may occasionally use a tape of different types of background music during Readers' Theater.

9. After students participate in Readers' Theater, a class discussion can be held about the success of the program. Readers can describe how they made decisions, the audience can respond to what was and was not effective. Plans for revision can be made.

Resources

Busching, B. (1981). Readers' Theater: An education for language and life. *Language Arts, 58*(3), 330–338.

Readers' Theater Script Service. P.O. Box 178333, San Diego, CA 92117.

Sloyer, S. (1982). *Readers' Theater: Story dramatization in the classroom.* Urbana, IL: National Council of Teachers of English.

Reference

Strategy description from: Harste, J., Short, K. G., & Burke, C. (1988). *Creating classrooms for authors.* Portsmouth, NH: Heinemann. 329–331.

Readers' Theater supports the students who are struggling with fluency. As I listened to their conversations about the text, I could tell that their comprehension of the story deepened. I'm looking for more stories that lend themselves to Readers' Theater. Any suggestions?

Pat

November 8

Dear Pat,

What do you think about the teachers performing Readers' Theater for the children during National Library Week? We could adapt some of the kids' favorite stories into scripts. My group loves *Anansi and the Moss Covered Rock,* and it's a perfect book for a project like this. Let me know what you think.

I love reading aloud to the kids! It's wonderful to hear their responses to the stories I share with them. I'm sometimes surprised by their insight and their questions. I have also begun to read short chapter books to the kids. Our favorite so far is *Wolf Story.* It's wonderful reading, and the kids love to predict where the tale will lead.

I'm struggling with literature groups, and managing the Reading Workshop portion of the day is something I need to work on. My daily schedule looks like this:

Half-day Kindergarten—8:30–11:00 a.m. & 12:00–2:30 p.m.
Sign-In
Morning jobs and Journaling (15 min.)
Large Group Circle Time (20 min.)
Calendar, Songs/Fingerplays, Conversation
Small Group-Sharing Time
Reading Workshop—Independent and Shared Reading (25 min.)
Book Sharing (15 min.)
Large group meeting—Open Workshop (10 min.)
Open Workshop (40 min.)
Centers (writing, math, science, etc.)
Snack
Read Aloud by teacher (15 min.)
Pack-up for home

Do you have any suggestions for shared reading or know of a book/article I could read?

Sue

November 12

Dear Sue,

You might want to read *Talking About Books.* I found the stories of classroom teachers interesting and the book offers a variety of suggestions and highlights different ways to use literature in the classroom.

It's exciting to use these "real" books to teach reading. I find myself looking to books to teach the strategies that I used to find in workbooks and worksheets. I notice that the kids' choices in literature have been influenced by the books I read to them. They are eager to take books home at the end of the day.

Pat

Reading Strategies in Kindergarten and First Grade

Each morning during Circle Time, the kindergarten children volunteered to share their responses to the books they took home the night before. Often, a parent, sibling, or babysitter reads aloud; sometimes the child reads to the elder instead! In the beginning of the year the responses resembled Book Talks, where children who wanted to recommend a book to classmates informally shared their opinions with the group. Students were invited to retell or read their favorite parts, or they shared drawings done at home the night before. A sign stating "Class Favorites" hung from the chalk ledge. A display of student selections invited children to read new titles and old favorites.

Once, while visiting a local bookstore, Sue noticed index cards hanging from the shelves of the adult fiction section. Employees were invited to share their recommendations with bookstore patrons. Having discussed the idea with the store manager, Sue went back to her classroom and invited her students to write their own recommendations, with the help of their fourth-grade "buddies." For several weeks, the recommendations of the children were displayed in the store, along with copies of the books.

At special times during the day, kindergartners could be seen lying on the rug in the reading center or on their nap mats, participating in Sustained Silent Reading. After the ten-minute session, the children gathered in small groups (3 to 4 children) to talk about the book(s) they had read. During the Reading Workshop, children selected from a variety of reading activities.

While Sue met with one reading discussion group, the other children listened to books on tape at the listening center, read chart poems and nursery rhymes with peers, dramatized a story using shadow puppets or the flannel board, or read alone or with a buddy on the rug.

In kindergarten, literature discussion groups centered around the sharing of and responding to good literature. Helping young readers develop a sense of story and to making connections with the world around them was possible when literature was used in the classroom. Children chose the books they wanted to read and talked about why these books were chosen. Initially, in Sue's class, literature discussion groups read the same book, each child had his or her own copy. After making predictions centered around the story, Sue guided the children through their reading experience. She asked them to predict events while reading and to discuss reasons behind their predictions. When predictions differed, readers anxiously "read on," looking for confirmation of their predictions. The group discussed the story's events as they unfolded. Content was examined, and the children were invited to respond to the text and pictures.

In the beginning, talk that focused on literary elements occurred on a basic level. After reading a book together, the group talked about characters ("Who was in the book?"), setting ("Where did the story happen?"), plot ("What happened in the story?"), and mood ("How did _____ make you feel?"). Sue recorded the children's ideas and opinions on chart paper hanging on the wall, placing each child's initials after his or her comment, prediction, or statement. After the group met a couple of times to reread and talk further about the book, focused activities/discussions were introduced to help the children begin to recognize and discuss different reading strategies.

In first grade, from the beginning, Pat immersed her students in a variety of predictable books, poems, and rhymes, enticing them with a variety of rich literature. Pat found that the choices her students made about books were strongly influenced by her own carefully selected choices. Pat also read for a short time each day from an inviting chapter book. She used this opportunity to demonstrate her own reading processes by using a think-aloud strategy. As she read aloud, she would stop and ask about the author's decisions, make personal connections, state opinions, or comment on well-crafted language or word choice. Pat also used think-alouds to demonstrate "fix-up" strategies and talk about her own miscues ("Oh, I think I skipped a word. Well, I'll just keep on reading and see what happens—maybe it won't make any difference. If it does, I can always come back to it later"). This led her first graders to notice and begin to talk about their own miscues. "Strategies" and "miscues" were common terms in Pat's classroom.

Reading Workshop time often began with reading an old favorite book, demonstrating to the children that it's good to revisit books we enjoy. It also offered students new opportunities to learn from books they may not have connected with in past readings. Sometimes Pat chose the book with a particular strategy in mind (e.g., predicting, using picture clues, using what is known to infer, or the use of alliteration to highlight a particular phonics/spelling pattern). Other times, she deferred to requests for an old favorite.

Reading Workshop continued with a Big Book, text set, or theme-related book selection. This marked an important transition for Pat. She began to look to trade books and Big Books, rather than the basal material and worksheets, for the instruction and strategies embedded in them. This was uncomfortable at first, but with time, she became a firm believer that every strategy and skill that children need to become proficient readers can come through the study of good literature.

Pat's classroom library grew quickly as she became an avid collector of children's literature. The wonderful books and stories that children enjoyed outside of school finally had their place in the classroom. They were no longer saved for special occasions or for extra time; they were now the core of the curriculum. The kids excitedly sorted the books into baskets, learning to distinguish between different genres as they did so.

During the last half hour of Reading Workshop time, a small group of students might have direct instruction from Pat, always with the idea of using a specific skill or strategy to comprehend what they are reading. This was also a time

---

Miscues, Not Mistakes

Teachers used to think that when readers deviated from print—substituted, omitted, inserted other words, and so forth—they were simply making mistakes and that was an undesirable thing to do. Ken Goodman convinced us that readers never make simple mistakes; instead, they make informed decisions based on the information in the text and what is in their heads. More than 30 years ago Goodman devised a series of naturalistic studies to discover what readers really do and what influences them to produce unexpected responses. What Goodman saw were readers of ALL ages and developmental levels using many different sources of information to help them produce something meaningful. As a result of this research, Goodman coined the term "miscue" to emphasize the idea that readers do not produce random errors while they are reading. Rather, they attempt to coordinate a number of different cues simultaneously to help them predict what they are reading. It is this process of prediction and cue orchestration that sometimes produces unexpected responses or miscues. No reader, no matter how proficient, produces word perfect reading all the time.

Source: Crafton, L. K. (1994). *Challenges of holistic teaching* (p. 142). Norwood, MA: Christopher-Gordon.

Suggestions for Further Reading

Goodman, K. (1965). A linguistic study of cues and miscues in reading. *Elementary English, 42,* 639–643.
Goodman, K. (1973). Miscues: Windows on the reading process. In K. Goodman (Ed.), *Miscue analysis: Applications to reading instruction.*
Goodman, Y., Watson, D., & Burke, C. (1987). *Reading miscue inventory: Alternative procedures.* Katonah, NY: Richard C. Owen.

when Pat asked children to engage in a Process Share, telling one thing they noticed about their reading. While this was going on, other students might read alone or with a partner, draw a picture about a book they had heard or read, or work at the listening center. There were almost always a few students who were happily singing or chanting along to a song or poem that was hanging somewhere in the classroom.

November 23

Dear Pat,

    I feel more comfortable using literature with the kids. I was looking for additional ways for the children to reflect on their nightly reading. After reading about literature logs, I decided to modify this approach for the kindergartners. When a child checks out a book to read at home, she writes a response to the story in a child-made "lit log." We just staple several pieces of paper together to make the log. The children usually write or draw in their lit logs and sometimes parents get involved by writing dictated responses in the logs. It's working so well! These entries are shared in small groups during Reading Workshop. The kids often recommend books to other children in their responses. I've started reading Donald Graves' and Lucy Calkins' books on writing. Maybe we can move in this direction after the holidays. Whew! I need a break more than the kids do!

                                     Sue

In the Spring, at the Zoo . . .

"Hey, look, Ms. Riordan, a suggestion box!" shouted Alyson.

"Just like the one in our classroom."

"Oh, we *have* to make suggestions."

"I have one," said Adam. "I think the lions need more room to run. They looked awfully bored."

"I think so too."

"Yeah, write that down."

With encouragement from his classmates, Adam proudly scribbled his concern for the encumbered-looking lions in his best invented spelling.

"How does this sound? Does it make sense?" As he did in the classroom, Adam looked to his peers for advice about the content and mechanics of his written message.

"You need a period at the end of this sentence." "And don't forget to write your address so they can write you back." Adam made some quick revisions and dropped his heartfelt message into the suggestion box.

April 12

Dear Sue,

    Can you believe this story about the suggestion box? I had to tell you right away. It was so impressive because the kids initiated it—not me. These are the kinds of out-of-school behaviors that tell me our real-world focus this year was the right thing to do! Watching this interaction at the zoo today strengthened my belief that literacy isn't a skill practiced in isolation, but rather, an ability (or a way of looking at the world) that comes about when kids think of themselves as *real* readers and writers. Today showed me once again that children can control their own literacy development!

Excited and confirmed, Pat

April 13

Dear Pat,

    I continue to be impressed by the language stories you share. The dialogues we've shared have helped me to be more reflective of *how* my students are learning. Even though this year has been a struggle (have you ever done this much *thinking* in your life?), it's been well worth it! I learned so much by watching the kids in my class and discussing their learning process with you and other teachers. Thanks for your ongoing support!

Feeling smart & supported, Sue

Reflective Commentary

Sue Smeaton tells the story of her nephew, Jack, who was immersed in literature all through his preschool years. Long before kindergarten, he had favorite authors, talked extensively about books with his parents, and saw himself as a reader. On the first day of kindergarten, he walked hesitantly into the unfamiliar classroom, looked around, spied a familiar Eric Carle book, spun on his heel, and called to his mom, "Hey! I think I'm going to *love* it here!"

For Jack, Eric Carle's books were a part of home in a new and possibly scary place. School began as an extension of a warm, loving home environment filled with good books, purposeful conversations, and a teacher who knew how to value children's talk and their need to be immersed in meaningful communication. For Jack (because we know the story of his primary years), school was a time where a knowledgeable professional moved his solid literate and language foundation forward by building on the experiences that he brought with him.

In their kindergarten and first-grade classrooms, Sue and Pat thoughtfully struggle with many of the key issues related to emergent literacy: extended opportunities to talk and listen, readiness, restructuring the curriculum to reflect children's needs and interests, authenticity (experiences that mirror the real world of people and language), support from older students as well as the teacher and each other, spelling, skills, strategies, literature, and how to address parents' concerns about a new way of teaching. None of these struggles is as important, though, as their concerns about starting with a child's existing language and knowledge and moving forward from there.

Pat and Sue focus their concerns about creating a more meaningful curriculum for their students by asking, "What is important to *them?* What real life experiences have they had, and what will they encounter? How can we continue the learning they were involved in during the years before we knew them? How can we support their meaning-making efforts in a complex world?" Considering what is natural and purposeful from a child's perspective is not an easy position to assume, but it is essential if our students are to go beyond "playing school"—if they are to see school as something more than being involved in someone else's game. Too often, smart young children come to us only to encounter a curriculum that is "dumb" (Cooper, 1993). Sue and Pat assume they have much to learn from all of their students; they work hard to walk in their shoes and consider reading, writing, and talking from the children's perspectives.

Talk

Talk is basic in any community—home, school, or work. As teachers, we hope that children have people in their lives who are willing to slow down, listen as they talk, and make them feel as if the world would stop if they didn't have a chance to express what's on their mind. We all know, though, that many of our students come to us without the benefit of sensitive adults who truly listen to their stories. But all children come with a great need to talk. In primary classrooms, we need to create opportunities for them to talk and to tell their stories. Linda Shepherd (1990, p. 73) says, "In our kindergarten we read and talk, think and talk, work and talk. We talk to ourselves and to each other, about ourselves and about each other, and with ourselves and with each other."

Sue and Pat reflected on Sharing Time, a common component in primary classrooms. They found that the children were often hurried, and they learned that significance could be masked by inexperience in fleshing out a narrative structure for an anxious audience that had not shared their own events. Moffett and Wagner (1976) suggest the same idea that Pat came to, that of dividing the class into small groups. This way, children can engage in extended talk, and clarification can occur through informal questioning. In "What is Sharing Time For?", Cazden (1994, p. 79) argues for heightened sensitivity in teachers. "Teachers, like physicians and social workers, are in the business of helping others. But as a prerequisite to giving help, we have to take in and understand."

Predictability, Readiness, and Emergent Literacy

Goodman states that "one of the things that's most important in early reading material, maybe the only really important thing, is its predictability. Children have to find what they're looking for, what they expect to find. So the text has to be predictable in terms of ideas, concepts, language, whatever" (1982, p. 5). Children find what they need to find, what they expect to find when we make familiar songs, rhymes, chants, or predictable books available. They find exactly what they expect when they have experiences (e.g., field trips, classroom speakers, group projects), and these events are captured in their own words in language experience stories. Young learners find exactly what they expect when they read the highly predictable language of books like *The Napping House, Jesse Bear,* and *Happy Birthday Moon.* Predictability is the reason Pat and Sue started with rhymes and songs and chants that the children already knew or could learn easily by singing and reciting together. Once a text is part of a child's oral language repertoire, making the oral-written language connection can become a joyful step.

Literacy is not a skill that children suddenly acquire at some magical moment because they have had enough direct instruction. It is an unfolding process, dependent on many rich, authentic experiences over time. The idea of literacy as an emergent process is in direct conflict with the concept of readiness, which implies that children have to develop a specific set of prerequisites before they are ready, willing, and able to deal with written language. Early childhood programs based on emergent literacy insights assume that children are "ready" for literacy from the time they are born. These curricula are based on the understanding that the accumulation of experiences and demonstrations over time creates proficient readers and writers.

Similar to Sue's "Kid Cafe" and phone area, primary classrooms that promote emergent views often provide real-world settings (already familiar to five- and six-year-olds) so that children may deal with the many authentic functions and purposes of print—there is real reason for a child to read or write when she takes a play food order, gives a traffic ticket to a five-year-old speedster, or writes directions for taking care of the class pet. In these classrooms, literacy is an integral part of the flow of the day rather than a separate instructional component.

While providing real-world settings *in* the classroom, teachers of young children also need to take them *out* of the classroom to highlight what they can already do as readers.

> If teachers take children for a walk around the school, the neighborhood, or a supermarket, they can get quick insights into the literacy kids have already attained. With a Polaroid camera a pictorial record can be brought back to the classroom. 'Show me anything you can read and I'll take a picture of it' is all the teacher needs to say. This sense of what they're reading is important for the teacher but it's also important for the kids who will discover reading isn't new, it's already part of their experience. (Goodman, Hood, & Goodman, 1991)

This is part of what educators mean when they talk about building curricula based on strength. Traditional curricula ask, "What is it that these kindergartners (first graders, second graders) *cannot* do? Where are the gaps in their learning?" In contrast, a primary curriculum built on strength begins by recognizing and uncovering what children *can* do, what they already know (and would like to know), and what contexts are familiar to them, and then moves forward from there.

As Pat and Sue note, Tom Eber was the principal at their school when they were making many of their transitions. Like Pat and Sue, Tom found himself becoming more and more reflective about the language arts instruction in their school.

"When I first walked into the school, there was a new basal series, complete with more worksheets and skill packs than I could count and every accompanying pre- and post-test available. The staff had no input or training with it, and there was simply an overall bad feeling in the school. K–2 teachers were frantically attempting to get through the levels and everything connected with them. It set up a terrible competition that no one could win, least of all the kids. There was very little time to read quality literature to students and no time for them to read it themselves. We had to make a change—and fast."

Besides experimenting with predictable books by reading them to his own children, Tom began to examine the professional literature himself. He also began sitting in on graduate reading courses at the local university, and began inviting the primary children into his office to share their writing and their favorite literature. Now the school had the major administrator and a core of teachers thinking, talking, and pulling together to transform a material-driven curriculum into a process, child-centered one. Tom contends that administrators must get intimately involved in some way. "It can be through collaborative exploration with teachers, as we did, by watching the process unfold through the reading and writing of your own children (which I was also lucky enough to do), or by making sure you are an active participant in school inservices just as the faculty is expected to be, but it has to be a group effort where everyone understands what the complex changes are all about. How can I respond to what teachers are doing if I don't look at it from the inside?"

Phonics

As Tom, Pat, Sue, and other teachers in the school struggled to make changes, they were repeatedly confronted with the quintessential question of phonics. Sue started her kindergarten program with the time-honored "Letter of the Week." Although she felt it was a better method of organizing curriculum than using the worksheets, she still questioned the validity of "centering everything around the letters" instead of around the learners in her classroom. Sue's reflections and conversations with Pat eventually moved her curriculum to a totally different plane, since she realized that the beliefs about literacy development on which Letter of the Week were founded have little to do with real language learning:

> Letter of the Week is built on the premise that letter recognition and their sound relationships form the primary knowledge base that all young children must have. It has seemed logical to find the smallest parts of reading/writing and assume that these must be taught first. It has also been popular to assume that young children don't have much or any of this knowledge when they come to school. In light of new understandings about preschool literacy, however, we have found that these basic assumptions don't quite hold up. Emergent literacy perspectives have helped us move in a very different direction and have given us new knowledge that encourages a reexamination of old views. (Crafton, 1994)

Researchers like Harste, Woodward, Burke, Taylor, Goodman, Teale, and Sulzby have helped us understand that young children naturally begin to recognize and understand print as they are intimately involved in the ongoing social situations of their lives. Daily life is filled with print in a literate society, and children, like everyone else, encounter it at every turn and begin to sort it out as they go. Young children are constantly engaged in the complex process of making sense of their worlds, and the printed word is an integral part of that. "The learners themselves have exploded our assumption about part-to-whole learning, forcing us to reconsider teaching *anything* in isolation and demanding that we rethink the notion of preschoolers coming to school as blank slates. The bottom line is that we are looking at pretty sophisticated learners when those kindergartners peek shyly around the corner to take a look at their first 'real' classroom" (Crafton, p. 106).

As Associate Executive Director of NCTE, Karen Smith gets many calls from the media to discuss the differences between phonics and whole language. While she refuses to address the topic in that form, she tells them she will be glad to discuss the role of phonics *in* whole language. Her response has an immediate clarification: Whole means whole, and phonics, as we all know, is part of the linguistic whole. No one deals with the letter/sound issue better than Mills, O'Keefe, and Stephens in *Looking Closely: Exploring the Role of Phonics in One Whole Language Classroom*. In Tim O'Keefe's first-grade classroom, phonics is dealt with in the same way all parts of language are—as they occur and as they are needed within authentic reading and writing experiences. The entire book is filled with examples of how he creates a classroom environment that nurtures the development of sound/symbol relationships and how he directly and indirectly helps the children in his classroom learn about phonics. Some of Tim's major curricular components include:

1. **Sign-in Journal.** The journal features student attendance patterns and documents the children's development over time in their ability to write

their names. It also serves as a forum for children to learn about the letters and sounds in their friends' names. Children make frequent observations about similarities in names: "*Charles* and *Chiquita* both begin with the letters *ch*." "*O'Keefe* has two *e's*, like *Kareem* and *green*."

2. **Name Game.** Tim devised a game that encourages the children to make predictions using their knowledge of letter-sound relationships in conjunction with their friends' names. They connect their personal knowledge and interests with graphophonemic concepts by uncovering consistencies and inconsistencies in language.

3. **"ABC Blues" and "ABC Rock."** Children learn the alphabet in the context of two popular class songs. Children often refer to the class-made alphabet cards above the chalkboard while playing "air guitar" and singing in rhythm to the teacher's guitar.

4. **Class Strategy-sharing Sessions.** Tim shares the effective strategies he sees the children using. For example, Kareem skipped the word *sweater* when reading his teacher's message, then went back to self-correct his reading when he read the clue embedded in the sentence, "It has a *V* on it." Kareem's sweater did in fact have a large *V* on the front of it, and Kareem strategically used this information to make sense of the sentence and to figure out the word *sweater*.

5. **Quiet Reading Time.** The children are encouraged to read a diverse range of materials in order to develop sensitivity to the various forms and functions of print. They use a pointer when reading big books, thus focusing on the relationship between the written and spoken word and on the rhythm and flow of language. As Tim listens, he informally monitors their strategies by reflecting on their miscues. For example, Ray discovered that his name was embedded in the word *crayons*. Vania substituted *Zam*, her brother's name, for *Zans* in a Dr. Seuss book. She self-corrected her miscue, and Tim indicated that he understood that she did so because the words almost look alike since they both begin with *za*.

In Tim's, Pat's, and Sue's classrooms, like thousands of other K–2 classrooms around the country, children are learning phonics as they are immersed in meaningful experiences. They are, as Smith points out, learning about phonics *in* language; they are learning that phonics is only one of many strategies that can help them as they read and write.

For many children, the school world of reading, writing, and talking is anything but real. When children can find no immediate purpose or connection to the learning of the classroom, we teach them that school is one thing and the real world is another. As Sue tells us, real-world learning in the classroom is a standard totally worth the struggle.

Remember Kate? She's the first grader in Pat's classroom who brought in the caterpillar which initiated a lengthy interdisciplinary experience. Kate is now in middle school and recently moved to a different district. She has strong memories of her primary years:

> When I was in the primary grades, I loved to read and write. My teachers gave me so much freedom as to what I wanted to read and write. My favorite time of the day was "journal time"—it was always a block of time where nothing could interrupt it. I'm so amazed as I look back that I was able to write as well as I could. I always wondered why my parents kept my

work. I could understand report cards, but every single little piece of paper that had to do with reading and writing? Now, I'm so glad that they did. I can remember feeling how important all of that was to me at the time.

As I grow older, I miss a lot of the activities we participated in as a class. Here at my new school there are a lot of things to get used to—such as, in rough drafts my thoughts have to be more clearly defined. During my years before transferring schools, my teacher or another student would explain to me what was unclear or needed to be developed further, whereas now most rough drafts have to be turned in and if something doesn't make sense I have red pen notes and marks all over my paper that are more confusing than the writing error itself. I try to avoid putting underdeveloped ideas into my drafts where in the past I felt comfortable knowing that someone would give their input or I could decide to leave that thought out of the piece. Just the other day I was given an assignment and this is what the chalkboard read: "Write a five paragraph essay about the relative of your choice. Organize your paper like this: 1st paragraph—Introduction (2–3 sentences), 2nd paragraph—Physical description (4 sentences), 3rd paragraph—Personality (4 sentences), 4th paragraph—Why s/he's important to you (4 sentences), 5th paragraph—Conclusion (2–3 sentences).

Working in the primary grades, I could develop characters, themes, and paragraph structures. Now, my freedom is limited. My projects are defined when they are assigned. At my age, my freedom is already limited. I have many rules that are not my own. Writing should be my chance to express myself without the interference of others.

My early reading experiences have influenced my love of reading and writing tremendously. In first grade, we read *The Very Hungry Caterpillar*, and just after that my Grandma brought me two caterpillars, so I brought them to school. My teacher developed a whole unit around that! I used to write my own books based on the ones we read in class.

I am extremely grateful to all of my primary teachers. I can't describe how important and special each tool was that my teachers used and I give them full credit for my skills now. They taught me a lot that I will keep with me always. One thing I will never forget is when they gave me the chance to make my own decisions as to what I wanted to write, it might sound like a little thing but I know that at least with me the quality of my writing is a lot better if I am writing a story that I brainstormed myself.

Kate Eber
September 1995

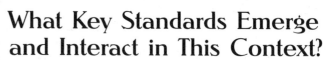

What Key Standards Emerge and Interact in This Context?

Students read a range of print and nonprint texts. Students read self-selected fiction, nonfiction, songs, rhymes, poetry, menus, and environmental print. They wrote, drew pictures, and received responses to their dialogue journals. They listened to and created their own oral texts during Sharing (Talking) Time.

Students read a range of literature in many genres. In both class-rooms, literature played a key role. Pat and Sue had daily read-aloud time exposing students to picture books, wordless books, poetry, nonfiction, and simple chapter books. Pat and Sue developed extensive sets of books that were related topically, thematically, by author, genre, etc. Every day, students had a chance to choose their own literature to read independently, with a partner or part of a choral reading experience. Readers' Theater was performed using many of the books from the classroom libraries.

Students apply a range of strategies. Through predictable books, teacher demonstration, and individual experience, students learned to use predicting as a critical reading strategy to help them comprehend and interpret stories. Students engaged in reader response activities by recording a range of responses (opinion, surprise, connecting to experience and other books, responding through art, etc.) in their journals and on large chart paper. Students noticed, labeled, and talked about the miscues they made during reading. They wrote their own predictable texts. Students varied their writing strategies and use of writing process as they produced different texts for different purposes—caterpillar observation journals called for quick note taking and often accompanying illustrations; message board writing had a personal, often passionate tone with a letter organization; suggestion box writing described a problem and possible solutions.

Students adapt conventions to communicate effectively. Students used a range of oral language conventions as they talked during Sharing Time, responded to literature personally and publicly, told personal stories, discussed the caterpillar, and placed and received orders at the Kid Cafe. Journal writing, message board notes, literature responses, and story writing gave students the opportunity to explore writing conventions as they communicated with a variety of audiences including peers, parents, and teacher.

Students use knowledge of language structure, language conventions, media techniques, and genre. Students in Pat and Sue's classrooms experimented with multiple forms of writing: menus, stories, journals, notes, suggestions, predictable books, name-signing, signs, environmental print. As they created writing in different forms for different purposes, they explored spelling, grammar, and punctuation within each context. Students also used oral language to explore various structures as they told stories, read aloud, planned their "Kid Cafe," discussed caterpillar observations, and responded to literature. Art was also an expression students explored as they worked through meanings in art and used art to support their writing.

Students participate in a variety of literacy communities. Students in both kindergarten and first grade classrooms checked out books from their classroom libraries to take home for reading with parents and siblings. All students belonged to their individual class reading and writing communities as they listened and responded to a range of literature and nonfiction books, wrote and shared their own books, and listened and responded to peer and teacher writing. Students also belonged to "buddy" groups formed with students from older classrooms. "Buddies" read to one another, engaged in shared reading activities, extended from literature through art and related texts, and planned, reflected on, and critiqued their time together. The roles in each of these literacy communities evolved as younger members became more confident and independent in their reading, writing, and reflecting abilities.

Students use technological and informational resources. Students used a word processing program to create a class phone book, to write predictable books following an author's published structure, and to compose simple stories.

Students use spoken, written, and visual language to accomplish their own purposes. Students saw the parallels between the Suggestion Box in the classroom and the one at the zoo—they made their own observations and suggested a change in the zoo's operation. Parents reported that Pat's first graders became avid readers of environmental print outside of the classroom. When literature became the focus, there was also a pattern of independent reading at home.

References and Other Resources

Barnes, D. (1975). *From communication to curriculum*. New York: Penguin.

Cazden, C. (1994). What is sharing time for? In A. H. Dyson & C. Genishi (Eds.), *The need for story: Cultural diversity in classroom and community*. Urbana, IL: National Council of Teachers of English.

Cooper, P. (1993). *When stories come to school*. New York: Teachers & Writers Collaborative.

Crafton, L. K. (1994). *Challenges of holistic teaching: Answering the tough questions*. Norwood, MA: Christopher-Gordon.

Dewey, J. (1915). *Schools of tomorrow*. New York: E. P. Dutton.

Donaldson, M. (1978). *Children's minds*. New York: W. W. Norton.

Dyson, A. H., & Genishi, C. (1994). *The need for story: Cultural diversity in classroom and community*. Urbana, IL: National Council of Teachers of English.

Ferreiro, E., & Teberosky, A. (1982). *Literacy before schooling*. Portsmouth, NH: Heinemann.

Fisher, B. (1991). *Joyful learning: A whole language kindergarten*. Portsmouth, NH: Heinemann.

Goodman, D., & Curry, T. (1991). Teaching in the real world. In Y. M. Goodman, W. J. Hood, & K. S. Goodman (Eds.), *Organizing for whole language*. Portsmouth, NH: Heinemann.

Goodman, Y. (1983). Beginning reading development: Strategies and principles. In R. P. Parker & F. A. Davis (Eds.), *Developing literacy*. Dover, DE: International Reading Association.

Harste, J., Woodward, V. & Burke, C. (1984). *Language stories and literacy lessons*. Portsmouth, NH: Heinemann.

Heath, S. B. (1983). *Ways with words*. Cambridge, MA: Cambridge University Press.

Mills, H., O'Keefe, T., & Stephens, D. (1992). *Looking closely: Exploring the role of phonics in one whole language classroom*. Urbana, IL: National Council of Teachers of English.

Paley, V. (1981). *Walley's stories*. Cambridge, MA: Harvard University Press.

Taylor, D. (1983). *Family literacy: Young children learning to read and write*. Portsmouth, NH: Heinemann.

Teale, W., & Sulzby, E. (1986). *Emergent literacy: Writing and reading*. Norwood, NJ: Ablex.

Books and Stories Children Like to Dramatize

This is a sample list of books recommended by teachers who dramatize stories with children on a regular basis.

Vigananee and the Tree Toad, A Liberian Tale	Verna Aardema
Who Sank the Boat?	Pamela Allen
All Night, All Day	Ashley Bryan
Shiko and His Eight Wicked Brothers	Ashley Bryan
Mr. Grumpy's Motorcar	John Burningham
Hey! Get Off Our Train	John Burningham
The Grouchy Ladybug	Eric Carle
Bony-Legs	Joanna Cole
The Large and Growly Bear	Gertrude Crampton
The Legend of the Indian Paintbrush	Tomie de Paola
Play with Me	Marie Ets
Hattie and the Fox	Mem Fox
Chrysanthemum	Kevin Henkes
Ben's Trumpet	Rachael Isadora
Letter to Amy	Ezra Jack Keats
Geraldine's Blanket	Holly Heller
The Carrot Seed	Ruth Krauss
The Elves and the Shoemaker	Freya Littledale
Anansi the Spider, A Tale from the Ashanti	Gerald McDermott
Brown Bear, Brown Bear	Bill Martin, Jr.
Me, Too!	Mercer Mayer
Stone Soup	Ann McGovern
Show and Tell	Robert Munsch
The Relatives Came	Cynthia Rylant
Abiyoyo	Pete Seeger
The Napping House	Audrey Wood

Folk tales and legends often make for successful dramas and also expose the children to other cultures. Look in anthologies of Native American and African stories, such as *The Keepers of the Earth* by Michael J. Caduto and Joseph Bruchac and *In the Beginning* and *The People Could Fly* by Virginia Hamilton.

Source: Cooper, P. (1993). *When stories come to school.* New York: Teachers and Writers Collaborative.

CHAPTER FOUR

LANGUAGE, LITERATURE, AND MULTICULTURAL UNDERSTANDING

Before reading, consider . . .

- *What you know and value about your own culture and ethnic background.*
- *One friend you have or have had whose gender, race, or ethnicity is different from your own: How is this friend like you? Different from you? Why do you feel connected?*
- *What you know about the home cultures and languages represented in your classroom.*

Elliott read the first paragraph of an article on multicultural education:

> Contrary to popular belief, the people of the United States have not been homogenized in a melting pot. While we all share some common experiences, many of the diverse groups that make up the country maintain distinctive cultural traditions and experiences. It is a multicultural society. (Sims Bishop, 1987, p. 60)

"Right on," he thought. One glance around the room confirmed what Bishop was saying. Instead of one homogenous group, Elliott saw several little cultures in this second-grade, suburban classroom. One cluster of four Mexican seven-year-olds sat huddled examining something one of them had brought from home; several Korean American girls sat together; two African American students leaned toward each other, deep in conversation; and then there were the more familiar Anglo American faces scattered around the room.

Over the years that Elliott had been teaching in this school, the profile of his classes had begun to change. This year he had a more ethnically diverse group than ever before, and he knew he had to give more serious thought to the nature of his curriculum.

He was nervous about it. What did he know about Korean culture? Was it like Vietnamese culture? Did he really have to deal with it, since the students with Korean backgrounds were born in America? And what about his own

prejudice when it came to the Middle Eastern countries? It wasn't long before that American troops had been in the Persian Gulf. And what about Mexico? The Mexican children in his classes usually maintained a low profile. These students often were not in school year-round, since their fathers were itinerant workers who came from Mexico to tend the lawns of the wealthier families in the area. Just yesterday, Elliott had seen a crew taking a lunch break in the back of a van that carried them from house to house.

When there were only white faces surrounding him, it was easy to ignore the multicultural issue. Of course, with the changing profile in the community, his school had been talking about multiculturalism—they had had a few inservices, and he made sure his students read literature from other countries, but he felt it was not connected to any part of their lives and was only a token to his conscience. Several years ago he had realized that the girls in his classroom were sorely mis- and under-represented in the literature and basal stories he used. Often, they were marginalized or depicted as passive sideliners, while the boys in the stories made all the important decisions. He had worked hard to develop a set of literature that depicted girls and women as strong and resourceful people, and now he knew it was time to dig in once more.

The one idea that resonated from the inservice workshops was that this kind of teaching was not for "the others." If teachers hoped to create a classroom that would influence the development of caring, culturally knowledgeable citizens, then they had to find a way to value all languages and cultures.

It was the beginning of the year, and with careful planning, Elliott thought he could learn a lot from and with his students; with some luck, he could turn this multicultural classroom into a multicultural community where his students understood and appreciated each other. That was his goal; he wanted to try to make cultural issues a central part of his language arts curriculum. He felt he knew a little of the theory, but even less of the practical implementation of multicultural education, beyond a smattering of literature. He decided to jump in

Strong Women and Resourceful Girls: Books for Children to Grow On

Adoff, A. *In for Winter: Out for Spring.* Harcourt Brace Jovanovich, 1991.

Auch, M. J. *Peeping Beauty.* Holiday, 1993.

Bemelmans, L. *Madeline.* Viking, 1939.

Bjork, C. *Linnea in Monet's garden.* R & S Books; distributed by Farrar, 1987.

Booth, B. *Mandy.* Lothrop, Lee and Shepard, 1991.

Brown, D. *Ruth Law Thrills a Nation.* Ticknor & Fields, 1993.

Browne, E. *No Problem.* Candlewick Press, 1993.

Burton, V. *Katy and the Big Snow.* Houghton Mifflin, 1973.

Caines, J. *Just Us Women.* HarperCollins, 1982.

Clifton, L. *Three Wishes.* Viking, 1976.

Cole, B. *Princess Smartypants.* Putnam, 1986.

Cooney, B. *Miss Rumphius.* Puffin, 1982.

Fox, M. *Koala Lou.* Harcourt Brace Jovanovich, 1989.

Fox, M. *Tough Boris.* Harcourt, Brace & Co., 1994.

Henkes, K. *Sheila Rae, the Brave.* Greenwillow, 1987.

Heyward, D. *The Country Bunny and the Little Gold Shoes.* Houghton, 1939.

Hoffman, M. *Amazing Grace.* Dial, 1991.

Johnson, A. *Tell Me A Story, Mama.* Orchard Book, 1989.

Keats, E. J. *Maggie and the Pirate.* Four Winds, 1979.

Lurie, A. *Clever Gretchen and Other Forgotten Folktales.* Crowell, 1980.

McKissack, P. C. *Mirandy and Brother Wind.* Knopf, 1988.

Merriam, P. C. *Mommies at Work.* Simon & Schuster, 1989 (1961).

Minard, R. *Womenfold and Fairy Tales*. Houghton Mifflin, 1975.

Minard, R. *The Paper Bag Princess*. Firefly Books, 1980.

Piper, W. *The Little Engine that Could*. Putnam, 1930.

Ringgold, F. *Tar Beach*. Crown, 1991.

Riordan, J. *Woman in the Moon and Other Tales of Forgotten Heroines*. Dial, 1984.

Steig, W. *Brave Irene*. Farrar, Straus & Giroux, 1986.

Yolen, J. *The Emperor and the Kite*. Philomel, 1967.

Yolen, J. *The Girl Who Loved the Wind*. Crowell, 1972.

Zolotow, C. *William's Doll*. Harper & Row, 1972.

and see what he could do. In the meantime, he would talk and ask and read and reflect in his trusty teaching journal.

Elliott decided to start with one of his favorite strategies, "Me Boxes." He took an old shoe box off the shelf and started examining its contents: one worn Mets hat, one photo of him and his daughter barbecuing in the back yard, one of the many journals he had kept since junior high school. . . . He had not changed the artifacts inside for years, and now, in light of the transition taking place in his classroom, he wondered just how much an old baseball cap really said about him. What did he want his students to know about him? Personally? Culturally? What *was* his culture? He hadn't really given it much thought. When he considered other cultures, he realized that he loosely defined them by their differences in areas such as family rituals and celebrations, language and ways of interacting, the different roles of men and women, how children were treated, food, and religion. Now he felt he had a starting point. After some thought, those ideas did seem to be important dimensions of culture.

He knew that language was a key cultural issue, and he felt that if he could somehow imbue a sense of status about his students' home languages, he would empower them in a critical way. He started thinking of the dialect in his childhood home. He had grown up in a rural Kentucky countryside where his family's way of speaking, he knew, was not viewed in the most positive light, certainly not considered "mainstream" or standard English. He smiled, thinking of the article he had just read about British disdain of American English. His many years in a large metropolitan area had resulted in a gradual fading of that southern accent, but his family still spoke with what many people called a "drawl." Could he start with the dialect of his growing years and show his students the beauty of it? Maybe his mother would agree to send him an audiotape, or maybe he could find a book where the dialect was close to his own. Now, what else should he put in the box?

With great ceremony, Elliott gathered his students around and extended the box toward them. "In here I have some very important parts of my life. The things in here will tell you a lot about who I am." One by one, he displayed and described the items.

Me Boxes
Strategy Description

1. During the first week of school, the teacher brings a box of any kind filled with special, personal items to share with the class. The items should represent family, hobbies, ethnic background, and professional interests to give students a sense of richness and variation in the teacher's life. Items could include pictures of family, artifacts from vacations or special times, favorite books, objects that represent family holidays or rituals, sports items, statues, maps, diaries, or childhood mementos.

2. The teachers takes each item out of the Me Box and talks briefly about its significance.

3. At the bottom of the box is a story or description that includes the items and experiences shared. The teacher reads the text to the class. Copies can be made so each child can have the story to read independently or with a partner.

4. Students are invited to bring their own Me Boxes to class. Shoe boxes work well, because they are easy to get and don't hold so many items that the strategy becomes unwieldy.

5. Students share their boxes with the whole class or in small groups. Whole class sharing can be done over a period of days. While it can take a fair amount of time, sharing with the entire class is a highly effective way to start the year and to help develop a quick sense of intimacy and community. It also gives the teacher enormous insight into students' lives and interests.

6. Me Box stories may be written before class and read as part of the presentation, or students may write stories after sharing their artifacts. The closer the match between personal items and text, the more predictable the materials.

7. Me Boxes should be displayed in a central place along with the complete writing so students can browse through the boxes. Individual items in the boxes may also be used to tell or write more focused, extended stories or for paired interviews.

Reference: Crafton, L. K. (1991). *Whole language: Getting started . . . moving forward*. Katonah, NY: Richard C. Owen.

First, he took out a newly selected photo of himself with his daughter. This time it was one of her birthday celebrations. "This picture," he told them, "has an important story behind it. In our house, we have a special ritual that goes with every birthday, but we didn't start it until our daughter was born." He told the story and then talked briefly about the idea of families creating "culture" together, touching upon how having children creates whole new rituals. Next, he produced a medal that had belonged to his brother who had been killed in Vietnam. He answered the inevitable questions about how his brother was killed and the war itself, and then he highlighted the fact that his family had been involved in other wars. His father, for example, had served in World War II. Finally, he took out the book and tape his mother had hurriedly made and sent. He prefaced it all by saying that his mom's talk sounded different than his own, that this is what he had grown up with, and he'd asked her to read the book aloud on tape just to show them how wonderful she sounds and so they would know something of his childhood culture.

"Boy, she really sounds different than you do. Why don't you talk alike?"

"What does your mom look like?"

"I never heard anyone say 'picture' like that before!"

Elliott listened to all the comments and then said, "You know, we also have many other ways of speaking in our classroom, and we need to hear them all as often as we can so we can remember how beautiful each one is. Does anyone want to try to read the title of my mom's book in a different language or a different way of pronouncing the words?" In one form or another, sometimes with a little coaxing and always with elaborate praise, Elliott helped his multilingual class take the first small step in opening up to each other's languages and cultures.

"Your first homework assignment is to come up with your own Me Box. Try to put things in that show something important about you and your family. We'll spend next week sharing, about five a day. Let's draw names to see who goes first."

As Woonghee opened his box, Elliott could see that it was almost empty. He fingered the few items inside and, with a gentle prompt from Elliott, brought out a frayed picture of his father. "This is my father when he was ten years old." Everyone strained to see, and Elliott asked if he would mind passing it around. Anna was the first person to get a close look. "Hey, he looks just like you!" Woonghee's head shot up and he was smiling. Elliott noted that during the rest of his sharing, everyone could see his face and eyes. "Just a little validation," he thought.

Rachael was next. The first item in her box was a postcard from Italy. "This is where we went on vacation this summer—my great-grandparents were Italian—and this is the special doll I got while I was there—I collect dolls." Marta, one of Rachael's friends, asked Rachael to pass it around, but she said she was afraid it would get dirty. Next, she produced a picture of her with her father in his oak-paneled office and then a photo of her mother at the university where she teaches. Rachael then carefully lifted out a long, red satin jewelry box. "This is a gold watch that belonged to my grandmother, and now it's mine." Rachael told the story of her grandparents' dating, and showed the inscription on the back.

Elliott watched the response to Rachael's portrait of her life and family. Everything about her seemed to be privileged. He hadn't quite anticipated the marked contrast in socioeconomic status and parents' livelihoods. Was there some way he could tip the scales and try to equalize the playing field, if only in his classroom?

Kathleen's Turkey Fire Story (Oral Transcription)

Well, the day before Thanksgiving and my mom wanted to cook a turkey so it would be ready at dinnertime. We were going to to to church, but my mom said no, we're not going to church because if the oven has a grease fire or anything, the house will start on fire. So we stayed home and they put the turkey in the oven in a paper bag and part of it was sticking out and so it started a grease fire in the oven. My mom knew right away. She saw the flames coming out of the oven. "There's a fire," she shouted. So she's going into the cabinet, throwing all the cups onto the floor trying to get to the baking soda. And so me and Kris are outside freezing, saying, "Can we come in, can we come in?" My sister pulled me outside— I was five when it happened. So she was pulling me outside and we said "Can we come back in?" so she knocked all the cups down— the cups were all over the floor. My dad's running around and just panicking. He was really scared. So my mom finally threw baking soda on it and the grease fire stopped. "You can come in," she yelled. So we came in and we see all these cups laying on the floor. I did put the baking soda next to the oven. So that was that. The fire didn't go on top of the turkey—just around the turkey.

Rachael was followed by a procession of four Anglo children presenting their collections, all with family situations much like Rachael's; the class learned that many of the parents were professionals of one kind or another. Marco was last.

Elliott knew that Marco, like the other Mexican children in the class, was transient in the school because his family had come from Mexico to tend the lawns for the season.

He also knew that his father was not literate in English or Spanish, but his mother was fluent in both. So far, Elliott had not had much luck getting Marco to say anything in class, and he noticed that the boy kept his distance from all the other children. Marco showed a small replica of an Aztec shield and a wooden cross. Finally, from the bottom of the box, Marco partially lifted a photo; he fingered one edge, was quiet for a moment, then laid it back. "That's all."

"That's all?" Elliott said.

"Sí."

Elliott learned later that the mystery picture in Marco's box was of his mother, father, grandparents, and four siblings. He had decided not to show it because he was afraid someone would ask him about his father's profession; he would have to say he was not a doctor or lawyer, but a gardener, and that bothered Marco tremendously.

The Me Box sharing took three days longer than Elliott had planned, but he knew it was more than worth it. When the last lid was replaced on the last box, Elliott asked everyone to once again take their boxes out of their desks. This time he asked them to carefully choose one special item that had at least one story attached to it that they would be willing to tell. Alex's hand shot up: "But we already told about everything." "This time I want the whole story, not just a sentence or two. Remember the picture I showed you of my daughter's birthday? Well, I told you about our family ritual for birthdays, but I didn't tell you the story behind that particular picture. This was the day she turned thirteen. . . ."

Elliott had taken a storytelling class in the summer and was convinced of the value of oral stories. He also guessed that many of his students brought a tradition of storytelling with them, stories from their parents or grandparents. He felt that this could be one wonderful way to get language and culture situated in the classroom. After the selections had been made, Elliott paired the students and encouraged them to tell their stories.

The artifacts in the Me Boxes were a place to start, but as Elliott roamed the classroom noting the animation in some groups and the serious faces in others, he also noticed that one story led to another. He could easily see the linguistic, cultural, and just plain I-like-you potential of the children sharing stories from home. He didn't know, however, exactly how to tap into the stories of the children's lives, or how to keep them flowing. He wondered if every child would really be interested in storytelling. Elliott pulled out one of his books from the summer class, *When Stories Come to School*, and started rereading.

A few days later, Elliott asked his students what kinds of stories they liked to tell. Some of the boys yelled out: "Monster stories!" "Yeah, scary stories." He acknowledged their responses and then deliberately called on a few girls who were sitting quietly with their hands up: "Adventure stories." "Stories about the same character—like in a series."

"Do you have any stories about yourselves you like to tell?" Most hands went up. "When I was four or five . . ." "When I got my puppy . . ." "When it was my first birthday . . ." Elliott asked them to write down three stories about themselves that they might like to tell.

The next morning a large number of students came to school clutching pictures of themselves and talking excitedly about them. Elliott knew it would be a good idea to start the morning with stories. After a few stories, he grouped the children in threes and asked them to continue. This time, as he circulated, he noticed that the students whose first languages were not English seemed to have little trouble comprehending the stories and also little trouble telling their own, with the help of sweeping gestures, some pictures, and an audience straining to understand and connect. At the end of a long and noisy hour, Elliott gathered everyone around him and asked what they had learned about each other and what they had learned about themselves. The children had a question, too: When could they do this again?

"Even though I had not done it before, I knew the storytelling would somehow make my reading and writing programs better. The real, thunderous impact was what it did to help these kids really know each other and appreciate one another *individually*. I could see the cultural walls tumbling down."

All of Elliott's students spoke at least some English. He decided that one way to put his students in constant contact with each other's languages and cultures was to encourage storytelling and discussion in small groups, with a special focus on the multicultural literature he planned to read aloud to them or the books and stories they would read independently. Each time there were discussion opportunities, he encouraged culturally heterogeneous groups and challenged them to come away learning something new in another language. Many of the students were intrigued with this challenge, but for some reason, it was Rachael who became intensely excited about "becoming multilingual," a phrase she loved to repeat to her parents and people outside of the classroom. Once she had made this her goal, she actively sought out her Korean and Mexican classmates to ask how to say and write specific words and phrases. Toward the end of the year, she asked for help in authoring one book in Spanish and another in Korean.

Elliott began to feel that he wanted the ideas of culture, language, and storytelling to move beyond the walls of the classroom, beyond individual children. So, one day he announced to his class, "I've been thinking—usually in second grade I have a Star of the Week, where each person gets to bring in special things about themselves and display them in the front showcase. What I'd like to do this year instead is have a Star Family of the Week. Someone from each of your families—moms or dads or brothers or sisters or grandparents—could come in sometime during the fall and share with us something about your family life."

Elliott made this announcement just a few weeks into the start of school. It was the beginning of a steady parade of cultures through Elliott's classroom that lasted far beyond the fall. Some families were represented more than one time during the year, as different family members came to share various aspects of their cultures and ethnic backgrounds. The focus on first languages expanded as parents brought in books, letters, and family documents written in the home language and their own special family stories. Often, following these visits, Elliott would pick up on one issue and ask his students to explore it across cultures. Holidays, family celebrations, and rituals were given a strong focus throughout the year. During the year Elliott made many calls to his students' homes, families reluctant to visit the classroom, offering to arrange for transportation if needed. He reassured parents that being fluent in English did not matter, and graciously invited them to come and share a family story or something about the home culture.

When it was Amanda's turn for Star Family of the Week, her mother came in to talk about their ancestry and told an amazing story. Amanda's maternal great-grandmother's maiden name was Custer, and she was a direct descendant of General Custer of military fame. However, on her paternal grandmother's

side, there was a direct link to the Cherokee Indians! Had anyone ever heard the story of Custer's Last Stand? As Amanda's mother described the massacre, everybody sat motionless and every eye was glued to her face. After the story, Elliott asked if anyone knew any American Indians. No one responded. "I think they're all dead," Jordan offered. "What makes you think that?" "Well, I've never seen any except on TV, and they always get killed."

Elliott glanced around his transitioning, multicultural community. "I have an interesting fact for all of you—there are American Indian tribes all over our country, and people of Mexican descent are often part Indian. I guess many of us have more in common than we would ever have guessed."

In his reading about multicultural education, Elliott came across this quote:

> What we should be teaching our children is that race hatred is wrong, racial chauvinism is wrong, and racism is wrong. People are people. Cut us and we bleed. If we lose a child, we cry.... It is the job of public education to teach everyone, whatever their ancestry, that we are all Americans and we all reside in the same world (Ravitch, 1987).

Marco

Marco was moderately proficient in English, but he saw an ESL teacher twice each week. In addition, he attended a pull-out program three times each week for support in reading and writing. During a pull-out session with five other second graders, Marco fell in love with *Dear Zoo*. This predictable book provided clues throughout to the zoo animals hidden inside. At the end was Marco's favorite, a puppy in a basket. Marco announced that he wanted to make something with zoo animals. He and his teacher discussed the possibilities and decided on a mural. After days of drawing and finding just the right magazine pictures, Marco remarked that he needed to write all the animal names. He followed up with a letter:

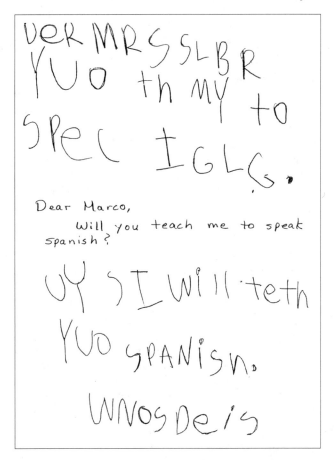

Translation:

Dear Mrs. Silvers,
Will you teach me to speak English?

Dear Marco,
Will you teach me to speak Spanish?

Yes, I will teach you Spanish.
Buenos días

Strategies to Decrease Gender Bias in the Classroom

1. Consciously extend your wait time (the average wait time teachers give students to answer a question is nine-tenths of a second!) to at least 3 to 5 seconds. More girls will be pulled into the discussion because they are often more thoughtful before they speak.

2. Several times a week at the beginning of class, give each student two poker chips. Whenever students want to ask or answer a question, they have to spend a chip. Everyone has to spend their chips before the class is over.

3. Make your students consciously aware of the research on gender bias. Ask students to start noticing whether girls or boys talk more in their own classrooms and who asks the most questions.

4. Notice who is speaking in the collaborative/cooperative groups in your classroom. Discuss the problem of one or two people (usually boys) doing all the talking. Develop class rules that help guarantee that everyone has a voice.

5. Tally how many times you call on or respond to boys versus girls. To achieve equity, distribution of attention should represent the proportion of each gender in the classroom.

6. Draw a class seating plan that indicates where each boy or girl is located in the room. Every time you speak to a student, make a check (or have an observer do this for you) on the chart to track each individual's participation. Study the chart to determine patterns: Is one gender receiving more attention? Who dominates and who is left out? Which areas of the room

Together Penny Silvers, the teacher, and Marco labeled the animals, first in Spanish and then in English. During these conversations, Marco told Penny that he had made both an American and a Mexican zoo—had she noticed the armadillo and the anteater?

After the mural was complete, Penny and Marco continued to trade language instruction, usually at the beginning or end of their time together. It was impossible to miss the pride that Marco felt when he taught Penny Spanish words. Penny began tracking down books written in English and Spanish, such as *Con Mi Hermano*, so they could read them together.

When Penny described the learning situation she and Marco had developed, Elliott was astounded. Even though Elliott had been encouraging first-language use in his classroom wherever he could, he had rarely heard Marco voluntarily say anything beyond "Sí," and Marco obviously considered that a slip, because it was quickly followed by "I mean yes." Elliott thought Marco was consciously censoring his first language. Elliott rarely saw Marco as the confident, self-initiating student that Penny was describing. Was there some way to expand Marco's role as a teacher of Spanish?

During the next session Penny had with Marco, she pulled him aside and, in low, serious tones, told him that he was such a good teacher, she didn't feel she could keep him all to herself anymore. Would he be willing to go into a kindergarten classroom and help them learn Spanish? She had discussed it with his teacher, who thought it was a great idea. Marco could use the time he had been spending with her to teach the kindergarten class instead.

The first day, Marco took his zoo animal mural and helped the kindergartners learn the names of their favorite animals. Penny stood in the back of the classroom and watched the slow smile on Marco's face as the children asked to learn about armadillos and anteaters. For many weeks after that, Marco went to the kindergartners twice a week. Like any good teacher, he tried to build his "instruction" around what they wanted to know—words of greeting, phrases they could use at home, their own names. Marco's reputation grew, and Elliott had requests from other classrooms for Marco to come and teach. The kindergarten teacher reported that her students were now speaking the Spanish words Marco had taught them to anyone who would listen. On the playground there were noticeable differences in the Hispanic/Anglo interactions; a little language knowledge had broken down some tough cultural barriers, and now many more Mexican and American students were playing together. Marco's increased status in the school was now undeniable, and Elliott began to see the ripple effect of Marco's stardom. Slowly, Marco's Mexican classmates began to receive teaching requests as well.

In January Marco left school to return to Mexico with his family for three months. For several days before he left, Marco had a visible sadness about him, but promised to bring back something special from his "Mexican culture" to share with his classmates. They, in turn, made him a goodbye book, written in both Spanish and English.

Reflective Commentary

Our children must learn to function effectively in a culturally and ethnically diverse country. While multicultural education has made some stunning strides in theory, research, and curriculum development, many teachers who teach in predominantly white classrooms as Elliott does don't always feel that multicultural education is a curricular perspective they need to think deeply about. Multicultural education is not ethnic- or gender-specific—it is not a curricular add-on designed only to support African Americans, Hispanics, women, or any other minority group (Banks, 1993). It is about educating within a democracy where learning to value diversity in opinion, religion, ethnicity, and race is a basic social principle.

Valuing First Languages

Just as multicultural education isn't just about minorities, multiculturalism isn't just about ethnicity: Home languages must be valued. "Teachers who wish to make use in class of the language resources of children will start by building the pride and confidence children have in their own language" (Goodman, 1982, p. 36). Even if we affirm a particular culture but disregard its native language, we have, in essence, drained the culture and the individual of its lifeblood. Ken Goodman has often said that if we take away a child's language, we have taken away the child's ability to learn. Even while just beginning to explore multiculturalism, Elliott found ways in his classroom to elevate minority languages and American English dialects to a different level than that found in society at large. In his classroom, it wasn't a matter of English being the only necessary language, the only language of voice and power. Every language in the classroom was seen as wonderful and unique; every language needed to be heard. Penny's brilliant decision to move Marco's teaching beyond her limited time with him immediately sent a message about the value of Spanish, at least in the school setting.

Sometime during the school year, one of Elliott's colleagues challenged his decision to encourage students to teach each other their first languages: After all, this is America, he argued, and students need to learn the language of *this* country. By this time, Elliott had seen the new strength in Marco and had heard reports of the changed social interactions on the playground. He paused for a moment, remembering that he, too, had once harbored this chauvinistic attitude. Then, in a tone that was close to a whisper, he said, "It's their greatest strength. How can I ignore that?"

There is an indescribable sadness about children who deny qualities in themselves that so distinctly define who they are. In *Raising a Daughter*, Elium and Elium explain that girls in our society are socialized into "relational behavior" (p. 6). That is, they "seek equal give-and-take, interdependent relationships, where people actively engage with each other" (p. 5). Girls tend to pursue ways of interacting that equalize power, rather than lauding power over others (Sadker & Sadker, 1994, call it "one upmanship"). The problem here is that many young girls too often lose themselves in the effort: "They give themselves away. To avoid causing pain or inconvenience to others, they swallow their own needs and feelings. Their loss of voice turns into resentment, eating disorders, rage, depression, low self-esteem, dependency, and sexual dysfunction" (p. 7). How many adult females shared this experience while growing up in classrooms where well-intentioned teachers simply overlooked them? Elliott noticed the same loss of voice with Marco, until Penny encouraged its reemergence through co-teaching. The sad part, as Jerry Harste says, is that Marco had to have even one moment of doubt about the validity, the power, and the wonder of his first language.

are attention-rich, and where are the dead zones, or places students can hide unnoticed?

7. Because boys tend to demand attention more than girls do, be careful about how you divert your attention away from a girl you may be speaking with when a demanding boy asks a question or requests your time. Send consistent messages to girls that say, "When I am talking to you, *you* are the important one right now."

8. Use literature that depicts girls as strong and resourceful people.

Reference

Sadker, M., & Sadker, D. (1994). *Failing at fairness.* New York: Charles Scribner's Sons.

Reyes, Laliberty, and Orbanosky (1993) report a similar phenomenon in David, a Chicano boy born in the United States. David's mother encouraged him to speak only in English, and as a consequence, "he interacted politely with everyone but never spoke Spanish" (p. 665). In this classroom, as in Elliott's, the students had ongoing opportunities to interact in linguistically heterogeneous groups. The article reports a significant change in David by the spring: "David began to feel comfortable with the Spanish speakers and with himself as bilingual; he even began translating for them! No doubt, the frequent use of Spanish in the classroom and the prestige accorded to bilinguals by both the Anglo and LEP (Limited English Proficiency) students contributed positively to his changing self-image" (p. 665).

The Need for Story

Elliott also effectively used oral stories to negotiate classroom culture and to guarantee that potentially unheard voices were empowered. In *The Need for Story* (Dyson & Genishi, 1994), the authors identify several reasons why stories, oral and written, produced by children, teachers, and professional authors are critical in all primary classrooms:

1. Children, like adults, use narrative to shape and reshape their lives, imagining what could have or should have happened, as well as what did happen.

2. Stories are an important tool for proclaiming who we are as individuals, and also as social and cultural beings.

3. Important relationships are established when stories are told.

Young children *need* to shape and control their complex worlds; they need ways to say who they are and what makes them unique and similar. Young children need close relationships and the feeling of belonging. Stories can do all of this.

Children need to tell stories simply for the sake of telling stories; the payoff in terms of self and culture and relationships is a boundless treasure in and of itself. But, as language arts teachers, we know the impact goes far beyond that into the world of reading and writing. There is a direct relationship between the stories of children and beginning reading and writing: When children are encouraged to construct and share their own stories, both oral and written, they

Multicultural Literature: A Few Good Titles

Adoff, A. (1991). *Hard to be six.* New York: Lothrop, Lee & Shepard.

Barbot, D. (1991). *A bicycle for Rosaura.* Brooklyn, NY: Kane/Miller.

Caines, J. F. (1988). *I need a lunchbox.* New York: Harper & Row.

Carls, N. (1991). *Wild, wild sunflower child Anna.* New York: Macmillan.

Cameron, A. (1988). *The most beautiful place in the world.* New York: Knopf.

Delacre, L. (1989). *Arroz con leche: Popular songs and rhymes from Latin America.* New York: Scholastic.

Greenfield, E. (1988). *Grandpa's face.* New York: Philomel.

Hedlund, I. (1990). *Mighty Mountain and the three strong women.* Volcano, CA: Volcano Press/Kazan Books.

Hoffman, M. (1991). *Amazing Grace.* New York: Dial Books for Young Readers.

Johnson, A. (1989). *Tell me a story, Mama.* New York: Orchard.

Lewis, R. (1991). *All of you was singing.* New York: Maxwell Macmillan.

Mendez, P. (1991). *Black snowman.* New York: Scholastic.

Paek, M. (1988). *Aekyung's dream.* San Francisco, CA: Children's Book Press.

Pomerantz, C. (1989). *The chalk doll.* New York: Lippincott.

Roe, E. (1991). *Con mi hermano/With my brother.* New York: Bradbury Press.

Soto, G. (1990). *Baseball in April and other stories.* San Diego, CA: Harcourt Brace Jovanovich.

Sneve, V. D. H. (1989). *Dancing tepees: Poems of American Indian youth.* New York: Holiday.

Steiner, B. (1988). *Whale brother.* New York: Walker.

Walker, B. K. (1988). *A treasury of Turkish folktales for children.* Hamden, CT: Linnet.

Yen, C. (1991). *Why Rat comes first: A story of the Chinese zodiac.* San Francisco, CA: Children's Book Press.

have the opportunity to explore the production of a narrative structure, to make decisions about what to say and how to say it, to begin to see how it all fits together to communicate their intent, and to experience firsthand the power of an interested audience response. Nothing can compare with a group, small or large, of valued friends leaning forward to hear your next words.

Burke (1978) suggests that each of us possesses a pool of language data. Information in the pool may enter as any language expression—listening, speaking, reading, or writing experiences—and may exit as any one of these expressions. Evidence for this conceptualization is easily seen as we observe children "borrowing" story structure from an author they have heard or read for presentation of their own stories, an indication that linguistic information (story schema) will be available for use in other settings as well. While Elliott had cultural harmony on his mind when he initiated storytelling in his classroom, he later saw how it gave his language arts program added life by elevating speaking, listening, and storytelling to a new curricular height.

The issue of helping children acquire more positive feelings about other racial groups is a complex one. Banks (1993) reports some startling research about the development of racial attitudes: "By age 4 African American, white, and Mexican American children are aware of racial differences and show racial preferences favoring whites" (p. 27). Banks's response is to suggest an "equity pedagogy," defined by the use of learning and cultural styles of diverse groups and by the use of cooperative learning, in which students of other racial and linguistic groups are involved. How do we, as teachers, embrace such a lofty standard when many of our efforts in that direction are clouded by our own lack of understanding of other cultures, other languages, and other views of the world? Edelsky suggests that one way is to begin to understand the relationship between language and power (1994, p. 255). Beyond that, she suggests raising cultural consciousness by consistently asking identity questions about the stories children tell and read in the classroom. For example, while reading the stories and studying the social studies materials about Pilgrims and Indians, one teacher kept these questions in front of her students:

- Who wrote this?
- Whose idea is this?
- Do you think this is the way the Indians would tell it? (p. 257)

Edelsky suggests that we extend those questions to make the issue an ongoing classroom inquiry, "the issue of whose story is being told here, and who benefits, and how they benefit from *this* version of the story being the one that is told" (p. 257).

As educators, we have to engage in our own critical literacy. As Shannon suggests, we must consciously step back and consider what *is not* being said, look for bias, and teach our students to ask questions about the social views perpetuated in the books they read. Fortunately, there are many picture books that we can use with our kindergartners and first and second graders which encourage them to begin to think critically about the perspective represented in stories.

Even at the primary level, teachers can begin to help learners see that knowledge construction is dependent on factors such as race, ethnicity, gender, and social class. One of our major understandings in reading in the last twenty-five years is that every interaction with print is an act of personal interpretation.

When readers express an opinion or present a certain take on a story, we can help them peel back the layers and understand its origins (Altwerger, 1994).

Elliott not only takes us into his classroom, but he also takes us into his thinking as he begins to address a complex educational issue. Elliott's approach to multicultural education is to first consider what he knows about culture, what observations he has made in his lifetime about the dimensions of culture (language, rituals, use of time and leisure, role of males and females, holidays, and celebrations), and then to move toward valuing diversity by starting with himself. Elliott operates on a tacit assumption: If he can understand and see the beauty of his culture (including his language) while viewing it as only one alternative among many, he can better help his students appreciate theirs and raise the status of minority groups in his classroom.

Starting with and then expanding personal experience can help enormously in understanding our own thinking and the perspectives of others. In a recent article, Flood, Lapp, Ranck-Buhr, and Moore (1995) share the impact of a literature discussion group in which teachers read and responded to contemporary fiction with multicultural themes. Many educators in the field of multiculturalism discuss how imperative it is to come to terms with personal views about cultural similarities and differences (Banks, 1994; Hodgkinson, 1991). The literature discussions met once a month and had a profound impact on the participants' classroom practices:

1. They gained personal insights that influenced their interactions with their colleagues.
2. They gained personal insights about the ways in which their growing knowledge of various cultures influenced how they treated their students.
3. They gained personal insights into the teaching and learning of literature.

In relation to the third point, these teachers make a stunning shift: "We began to manage our literature instruction in a way that more closely resembled our book club format. We allowed more time for discussion, realizing that *meaning making is based on hearing many voices*" (italics mine, p. 722).

What Key Standards Emerge and Interact in This Context?

Students read a range of print and nonprint texts. Students read fiction and nonfiction material that represented diversity in gender, social class, and ethnicity. They listened to and told family stories and rituals. They made connections among thematically and topically related books about different cultures, holidays, and customs.

Students read a range of literature in many genres. Elliott made the development of a multicultural literature classroom library a professional goal. Students were surrounded by books that represented ethnic, gender, social, and cultural diversity. They had daily opportunities to listen to and read independently from these selections.

Students apply a range of strategies. Students used a variety of verbal and non-verbal cues and strategies as they listened to and told stories to classmates whose first language often differed from theirs. Rachael used topic selection, drafting, peer conferencing, revising, and editing strategies to produce an English/Korean book. Marco developed a core of reading, writing, speaking, and teaching strategies as he communicated with different audiences for different purposes—e.g., letters to Penny, creation of a zoo mural, reading and writing predictable books, telling stories, and teaching kindergartners and peers simple vocabulary and sentences in Spanish.

Students develop an understanding of and respect for diversity. Students interacted within culturally and linguistically diverse groups as they told individual and family stories. Family members from various backgrounds and cultures came into the classroom to share their language, customs, and ways of thinking and dressing. Students read and discussed a range of multicultural literature—they were able to see themselves and their home communities in books as well as their classmates from different ethnic backgrounds. Students developed different and more ethnically diverse social patterns within the classroom and on the playground.

Students whose first language is not English use their first language to develop competency and understanding. Students told personal and family stories that included words, phrases and whole sentences from both English and their first language. Marco and other Mexican students taught peers and younger students words and phrases in Spanish. Students listened to cultural information and family stories in English and the language of the culture being spotlighted. Students used their first language in combination with English to discuss and comprehend literature with their peers and the teacher.

Students participate in a variety of literacy communities. Elliott's students belonged to a number of different storytelling and literature groups throughout the year. Individuals brought personal expertise by sharing family stories and rituals and contributed interpretations and explanations of culturally relevant fiction and nonfiction. Marco belonged not only to his classroom community (a role which changed significantly as he began to "teach" in and out of the classroom) as a reader/writer/storyteller, but also as a knowledgeable member of his resource program community and as an itinerant teacher in the kindergarten classroom. Even when he returned to Mexico, Marco remained a contributing member of his classroom community by selecting cultural artifacts for them. Every student connected their home culture with the classroom community by sharing artifacts that profiled their families, ethnicity, and first language.

Students use spoken, written, and visual language to accomplish their own purposes. Some parents told Elliott that, on family trips to the library, their children were requesting literature that reflected the cultures of the classroom. Marco actively looked for cultural artifacts to share with his classmates on his return from Mexico.

References and Other Resources

Altwerger, B. "From personal response to social reflection: Literature as critical reflection." Whole Language Umbrella Conference, Winnipeg, 1993.

Bank Street College of Education. (1992). *Explorations with young children: A cultural diversity curriculum guide.* Mt. Rainier, MD: Gryphon House.

Banks, J. (1993). Multicultural education: Development, dimensions, and challenges. *Phi Delta Kappan, 75*(1), 21–28.

Christensen, C. P. (1989). Cross-cultural awareness development: A conceptual model. *Counselor Education and Supervision, 28,* 270–287.

Cohen, C. B. (1986). *Teaching about ethnic diversity.* Bloomington, IN: Clearinghouse for Social Studies and Social Science Education.

Dyson, A. H., & Genishi, C. (Eds.). (1994). *The need for story: Cultural diversity in classroom and community.* Urbana, IL: National Council of Teachers of English.

Edelsky, C. (1994). Education for democracy. *Language Arts, 71*(4), 252–257.

Elium, J., & Elium, D. (1994). *Raising a daughter: Parents and the awakening of a healthy woman.* Berkeley, CA: Celestial Arts.

Flood, J., Lapp, D., Ranck-Buhr, W., & Moore, J. (1995). What happens when teachers get together to talk about books? Gaining a multicultural perspective from literature. *The Reading Teacher, 48*(8), 720–723.

Fyfe, A., & Figueroa, P. (Eds.). (1992). *Educating for cultural diversity: The challenge of a new era.* New York: Routledge.

Garcia, E. E. (1991). *Education of linguistically and culturally diverse students.* Santa Cruz, CA: University of California Press.

Goodman, K. (1982). The language children bring to school: How to build on it (1969). In F. Gollasch (Ed.), *Language & literacy: The selected writings of Kenneth S. Goodman, Volume 1.* London: Routledge & Kegan Paul.

Hatter, M. (1991). *The family experience: A reader in cultural diversity.* New York: Macmillan.

Hodgkinson, H. (1991). Reform versus reality. *Phi Delta Kappan, 73*(9).

Johnson, I. (1993). *Dealing with diversity through multicultural fiction: A library and classroom partnership.* Chicago: American Library Association.

Lambert, W. E. (1990). *Coping with cultural and racial diversity in urban America.* New York: Praeger.

Locke, E. W., & Hanson, M. J. (Eds.). (1992). *Developing cross-cultural competence: A guide for working with children and their families.* Baltimore, MD: Brookes.

Miller-Lachman, L. (1992). *Our family, our friends, our world: An annotated guide to significant multicultural books for children and teenagers.* New Providence, NJ: R. R. Bowken.

Nieto, S. (1992). *Affirming diversity: The sociopolitical context of multicultural education.* New York: Longman Press.

Ramsey, P. G. (1989). *Multicultural education: A source book.* New York: Garland Publication.

Ravitch, D. (1987). *The schools we deserve: Reflections on the educational crisis of our time.* New York: Basic Books.

Reyes, M. L., Laliberty, E. A., & Orbanosky, J. M. (1993). Emerging biliteracy and cross-cultural sensitivity in a language arts classroom. *Language Arts, 70*(8), 659–668.

Rigg, P., & Allen, V. G. (Eds.). (1989). *When they don't all speak English: Integrating the ESL student in the regular classroom.* Urbana, IL: National Council of Teachers of English.

Rochman, H. (1993). *Against borders: Promoting books for a multicultural world.* Chicago: American Library Association.

Sadker, M., & Sadker, D. (1994). *Failing at fairness.* New York: Charles Scribner's Sons.

Sierra, J. (1991). *Multicultural folktales: Stories to tell young children*. Phoenix, AZ: The Oryx Press.

Takaki, R. (1993). *A different mirror: A history of multicultural America*. Boston: Little, Brown & Co.

Tiedt, P. L. (1989). *Multicultural teaching: A handbook of activities, information and resources*. Boston: Allyn & Bacon.

Ycobacci-Tam, P. (1987). Interacting with the culturally different family. *The Volta Review, 89*(5), 46–58.

Multicultural Alphabet Books

Aylesworth, J. (1992). *The folks in the valley: A Pennsylvania Dutch ABC*. New York: HarperCollins.

Brown, R. (1991). *Alphabet times four: An international ABC*. New York: Dutton.

Edwards, M. (1992). *Alef-bet*. New York: Lothrop, Lee & Shepard.

Feelings, M. (1974). *Jambo means hello: Swahili alphabet book*. New York: Dial.

Hudson, W., & Wesley, V. W. (1988). *Afro-Bets book of black heroes from A to Z: An introduction to important black achievers for young readers*. Orange, NJ: Just Us Books.

Isadora, R. (1983). *City seen from A to Z*. New York: Greenwillow.

Mayers, F. C. (1988). *ABC: Egyptian art from The Brooklyn Museum*. New York: Harry N. Abrams.

Mayers, F. C. (1992). *A Russian ABC*. New York: Harry N. Abrams.

Musgrove, M. (1976). *Ashanti to Zulu: African traditions*. New York: Dial.

Rice, J. (1991). *Cajun alphabet*. Gretna, LA: Pelican Publishing.

Wells, R. (1992). *A to Zen: A book of Japanese culture*. Saxonville, MA: Picture Book Studio.

Zuill, J. (1980). *Bermuda alphabet book*. Bermuda, West Indies: Island Press Limited.

Source: Chaney, Jeanne H. (1993, October). *The Reading Teacher, 47,* 104.

CHAPTER FIVE

INTEREST GROUPS AND EVALUATION: CHILDREN IN CHARGE OF THEIR LEARNING

Before reading, consider . . .

- *A time when you successfully worked toward a common goal with someone of differing strengths and abilities.*
- *A major event in your life (e.g., work-related presentation, wedding, vacation): What issues did you reflect on before, during, and after the event?*
- *The degree to which you are encouraging students to value one another's strengths and contributions.*
- *The role reflection plays in your students' learning.*

Mrs. Vondrak, during the summer, I'm going to start researching about the planets because then I'll have some stuff for when school starts again, and I can share it with my interest group.

Yeah, and I'm going to Sea World in August, so I'll get some information for Alan's project about whales.

These were pieces of conversations going on at the end of first grade in Mary Vondrak's room as teacher and students planned to move together to second grade. Staying with the whole class for another year gave Mary an invaluable opportunity to continue building a community of learners and additional time to respond to their needs.

In first grade, Mary had successfully created a caring, connected, inclusive community of 26 learners, each with a wide range of interests and abilities. She knew them well through her extensive anecdotal observations, conferences, group interactions, literature discussions, integrated thematic experiences, and reflective talk. Penny Silvers, the reading coordinator, worked in the classroom with several of Mary's students. They were both astute "kid watchers," delighting in sharing observations and stories about the students. They both had high expectations that all the children would be readers, and responded positively to the students' approximations and ventures into learning. Their support of the emerging literacy was reflected in the many celebrations and shared talk about what the students were learning.

Problems and Possibilities of Moving to Second Grade

The principal was very supportive of Mary's move to second grade with her class, but in the planning process, a variety of questions and challenges emerged. One major issue involved administrative concerns about curriculum coverage and district outcomes, since the district had recently adopted learner outcomes which had a direct impact on curriculum and instruction. The expectations were that students would become effective communicators, constructive thinkers, self-directed learners, quality producers, and responsible collaborators. Along with concerns about implementing these outcomes, the principal had some specific questions she wanted Mary to address:

- How can you work within the grade level parameters and fulfill district expectations for second grade?
- If you take your first graders to second grade, how will you differentiate the curriculum and provide for individual differences?
- How can you ensure that the next year would be more than "First Grade, Part 2"?

Mary had her own questions and concerns:

- How can I continue to develop and sustain a student-centered curriculum, providing learning opportunities to meet the needs and interests of the diverse student population in my classroom, and still be accountable for meeting district expectations?
- How can I keep track of all the learning that is going on?

And then there were Penny's questions:

- How can I continue to support students with special needs within the context of Mary's classroom, helping them to be active, successful participants in that community?
- How can I best collaborate with Mary as we explore the benefits of staying with a class over time?

The ultimate challenge was to cover the curriculum while ensuring that Mary's students would continue to have choices in pursuing what they were interested in learning. As Penny and Mary planned for the coming year, a solution emerged to solve the dilemma of maintaining a student-centered classroom while trying to implement a grade-level curriculum: they would organize and support student interest groups.

At the beginning of first grade, they had both read an article by Joby Copenhaver called "Instances of Inquiry" (1992). This article provided information about implementing groups based on student interests and choices. In first grade, Mary's students had become familiar with the process of working together in small groups of their choice to research topics of interest. They were comfortable sharing information with each other and celebrating their learning through class presentations and projects.

Mary's experience with interest groups in her first-grade class helped her use them in second grade as a way to ensure that she would meet individual needs, connect to district content expectations, and keep ownership of the learning process in the students' hands. She continued to use the open-ended interest groups to allow the children to explore topics of their choice, but she also adapted them for use with grade-level curriculum. All the second-grade teachers were planning to study biographies, and this provided a perfect opportunity to use interest groups as a way of covering the required curriculum while still retaining student autonomy and flexibility.

Before starting the biography unit, a class meeting was held to reflect on the students' experiences with interest groups in first grade. They discussed what worked, the strategies that helped them learn, projects the students liked and why they were so successful. They talked about all that the students had learned from so many different interest group experiences:

> *J:* Our interest group on rocks was the best!
>
> *M:* Oh yeah, I remember that collection you brought in.
>
> *K:* Remember that chart you made about gemstones?
>
> *L:* Yes, and my dad came in because he's a jeweler.
>
> *J:* We sure learned a lot about rocks and minerals.

In this instance, biographies were the focus, and the students brainstormed all the famous people they could think of, past and present. A student recorder filled the board with names that were identified, and then they were categorized into broader groups, including everyone from famous women to astronauts. The students formed research groups based on their interests and began discussing what they already knew about the people in their category. After choosing a special person within their category, they listed some questions they wanted to know about that person, like these about Helen Keller:

Helen Keller

How did she become deaf and blind?

How old was she when she became deaf and blind?

Could she talk at all?

Did she get married?

How did she learn?

Then their thoughts turned to finding resources and information about the various people being researched. Because it was a study of biographies, they provided books as well as magazine articles, newspaper clips, and any other available sources.

The initial brainstorming, question asking, and resource providing took about three 45-minute class sessions. They began by setting aside three sessions per week for these groups, in addition to regular reading and writing time. Because the initial level of involvement was so unexpectedly high, Mary decided to make interest groups an integral part of the day, becoming the center of reading and writing time rather than an addition.

In this heterogeneous, inclusive, second-grade classroom, everyone was reading, talking, asking questions, sharing, and problem solving. Collaboration was a large part of the classroom culture. Students were helping each other, parents were invited to help students research, and resource teachers became part of the groups, working with all the children and not only those with IEPs. Interest groups provided a way of interpreting the second-grade curriculum so that it was meaningful to the students.

HELLEN KELLER

① Wehn Heelen was 6 mons old, she began talkig.

② Heelen usd her hans to taek.

③ Althgh seh was blind, she gratuatid frum college.

④ She wrote a book abut her life.

Helen Keller

Penny joined the group interested in learning about Helen Keller as a participant and support person for a particular special needs student. The four members of this group were deeply engrossed in the Braille alphabet and were trying to learn sign language with a speech/language pathologist, whom they had written to and invited to the school for lunch. Penny knew of a hearing-impaired class in a nearby school, so each student in the group wrote a letter to that class, including pictures, information about themselves, and questions about how they could "talk" through signing.

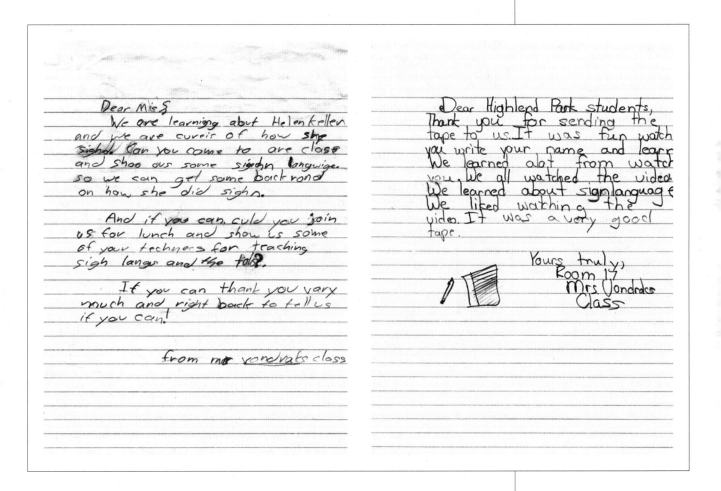

In return, the hearing-impaired class sent a video of themselves signing "hello," signing the alphabet, and telling a little about themselves, with narration by the teacher. The group was thrilled with this resource, and it generated a lot of talk about disabilities:

K: Wow! Their classroom looks just like ours.

D: What did you expect? They're just like us, they just can't hear.

K: Some of them can hear a little, I think. I wonder how they can talk?

D: Let's add that to our questions: How do deaf people talk?

M: Did you know that Miss America is deaf and she's a dancer? She can talk a little, I think. Maybe Mrs. Silvers can help us find out about her.

This video provided the impetus for many discussions about dealing with disabilities, and the entire class benefited from it. The Helen Keller group practiced signing at recess, at lunch, and after school. With Penny's help and some coaching from the speech/language teacher, they made a brief video to send back to the class as a thank-you, using sign language to communicate their names and tell something about themselves.

Literature group discussions were an important part of the learning in interest groups. The students loved reading the variety of wonderful fiction and nonfiction books in the text sets about their chosen subjects. The groups engaged in thoughtful discussion, asking insightful questions and referring to their reflective journal notes to expand their conversations. The conversations were so interesting and informative that Penny thought it would be a good idea to audiotape the discussions and play them back later for the group to analyze and share with the class.

They frequently joined the discussion groups as participants. It was especially hard to leave their "teacher voices" behind and enter the discussions as authentic participants, remaining quiet and listening, unless they had something important to contribute to the conversation. One instance with Penny stands out in particular. The students had read two chapters in *A Picture Book of Helen Keller*, by David Adler. The children used a bookmark strategy as a way of starting their discussion. They were sharing a question they had written down from the chapter they had read and talking about possible answers. As Penny joined them, the children were already into a lively discussion:

D: I can't believe Helen Keller locked her mom in the pantry.

T: Yes, and she cut off her friend's hair, too. How could she see to do that?

Penny: Well, haven't you done anything really naughty?

D: Mrs. Silvers, excuse me, we were talking about what Helen did! And it was really hard for her; she was blind! Maybe we can talk about what we've done, later.

They chuckled when they listened to the tape and realized that the students were right! Penny was trying to help them connect with their prior knowledge as a reading strategy, while they were involved in discussing a puzzling issue that came up in the story. It was not at all the right time for a strategy lesson. Their ownership in the process was so strong, they felt comfortable telling Penny to wait for a better opportunity to interact with them. They played the tape for the whole class as a part of a short lesson on what makes a good discussion, and this was so successful as a learning strategy, they continued to use audio- and videotape segments to help students reflect on their own learning and share their insights with each other.

The group decided to dramatize highlights from Helen Keller's life, using sign language to emphasize key phrases. The speech/language teacher was invited to join the group, and she helped teach the entire class how to sign their names. The students remained interested in this means of communication for a long time after their research was finished, using signing as a way to talk privately to each other or send messages across the room without disturbing the other children.

Country Music

Country music was special to Mary. One group was interested in performers and decided to learn about Garth Brooks. He was scheduled to perform locally in a few months. The students and Mary gathered magazine articles and newspaper clippings that highlighted his life story. Books on country music led to the development of an elaborate timeline of country music, ending with present-day performer Garth Brooks. Letters were written to a local radio station requesting any information, and the station played a request song dedicated to the class! A disc jockey was invited to come and talk to the class.

The assistant principal was a well-known music resource, and the group interviewed him about his feelings on country music and his opinion of Garth Brooks. This spurred the development of numerous surveys about country music, Garth Brooks, and his popular songs. These surveys were transferred to graphs and displayed. The group brought in tapes of Garth's greatest hits and Mary taught the students some simple line dances. It was not unusual to pass Mary's room during lunch time and see her students "stepping country."

Tim, a special needs student, took an active part in this group. In fact, it would have been hard to identify him as a student who needed extra support, as he was often the ringleader of the

group and his enthusiasm was so contagious. Tim was also the one who kept the group organized and remembered each child's topic and responsibilities. He loved to give orders: "Come on, you guys. We have to do this. You two, work on the timeline. Now, here's Garth Brooks. Start with him, and work backwards."

There were times when Tim had difficulty reading magazine articles or books. Classmates were quick to volunteer to sit in the hall and read with him. Penny, too, would work with him when she saw he needed information or help planning for his presentation. The teachers celebrated the time when Tim was so engrossed in reading his research, he shook his head and waved them off with his hands, indicating that he was too involved in what he was doing for anyone to bother him.

Tim's LD teacher met with him both in the resource room and in the classroom. By connecting the resource support with the classroom experiences, Tim was able to write a book about country music in the resource room and later share it with the interest group in his class. Tim also had a special interest in the guitar and, as his contribution to the final sharing of the group's information, he gave a performance for the class. This enriched the production, and it helped the children see his strengths and value him as a musical expert. The whole class applauded his accomplishment. They videotaped this group's presentation and played it often. It was a favorite rainy day request, and it was a big success for Open House viewing.

Oprah

Amy chose Oprah Winfrey as her research subject. This was of great interest to her classmate, Lisa, who had difficulty reaching out to other students and sharing. She had many idiosyncrasies and never quite fit. She seemed to live on the fringes of the classroom, not feeling good enough about herself to venture into the mainstream. Much to Mary and Penny's surprise, Lisa's interest in Oprah was so strong that she overcame her shyness and asked to work with Amy. Through their common interest in Oprah, the girls formed a relationship in which Lisa blossomed. Over time, the teachers noticed that she behaved differently, participating in group discussions, and even took on a new persona, as she became more self-confident and accepted as part of the group.

The girls gathered information for their project portfolio, which contained all the artifacts that they gathered, created, and wrote as they planned their presentation. There was a table of contents, and each piece had a reflection about why it was included. They were very selective about the artifacts they used. These included a timeline of Oprah's life, a web of her accomplishments, research questions and responses, interview questions, journal entries, poems, and more. They spent a lot of time creating a picture of Oprah for all to view. One of the girls' favorite selections was a pictorial collage of Oprah in her role as a talk show host. Their reflection about the collage said,

> Our pictures show Oprah as a talk show host. They also show her as a black woman who made a difference. We chose it because it really is Oprah!

The first piece in the portfolio was a letter of introduction inviting the reader to view their portfolio. They did it as a rap:

> Look inside and you will see
> All that Oprah chose to be.
> Her story is true
> And important, too . . .
> We do . . .
> Invite you!

The girls enjoyed learning about Oprah's interesting life story. They looked at the many ways Oprah makes a difference in the lives of others, and they were fascinated with the way she overcame difficulties in her own life. Their conversations were sophisticated as they explored broad issues dealing with gender and cultural awareness.

Lisa: Oprah had to work really hard to get into television and to become a big star.

Amy: Yes, it was harder for her because she was a woman.

Lisa: Yes, most of the jobs in TV and radio were men's jobs. It seems like you still see more men on TV today.

Amy: That isn't fair! Girls can do as good a job . . . better. Oprah proved that!

Lisa: Hmm . . . she had to work even harder because she was black, too.

When it came time to share the information with the class, the girls shared their project portfolio, and they also put on a performance using a talk show format. Amy first took the role of Oprah, then switched places and became her interviewer. Lisa helped write the questions and directed the production (complete with commercials!). This production was creative and entertaining, and it provided an opportunity for the girls to share their thoughts about important social issues with the entire class.

Collaboration, Reflection, Management, and Evaluation

Penny's official role was that of reading coordinator, working on reading and writing with several special needs students in Mary's room. Her unofficial role was that of collaborator, coresearcher, and fellow teacher, as they tried to capture and record all the learning that was occurring in Mary's room. Their questions grew with their collaboration:

- How do the students know so much about so many topics?
- How much are they learning from each other?
- What are they learning about their topics as they teach to each other?
- How is their talk and sharing impacting their learning?
- What strategies are they using?
- What do they know about themselves as learners, readers, and writers?

There were teacher management questions as well:

- How can the learning process be documented?
- How can mini-lessons be used to the children's best advantage?
- How much time should be spent in interest groups?
- What if a group is ready to share their information and the others are not?
- What happens when a group fizzles out?

They decided that process strategies needed to be highlighted so students would know that risk taking, collaborating, sharing, questioning, and thoughtful reflection were valued. This also connected to the broad learner outcomes developed in the district. The teachers knew that when they conferenced with students about their work and learning, it helped them recognize the significance of what they were doing as a result. Mary decided to try weekly mini-lessons to highlight various process strategies and raise the children's awareness of what they were doing as they were learning.

In addition, Mary and Penny paid attention to the kinds of questions they were asking the students and the positive responses they were giving them. For example, during conferencing times, they made a point of discussing strategies they noticed the children using that seemed to be effective: "I noticed that when you read your story to me, you went back and reread the first paragraph because you saw it didn't make sense, and then you changed a few words to make it more understandable. That's a *great* strategy to use. When you are reading and something doesn't make sense, take the time to reread it to see what's missing or different." The teachers hoped that this kind of instructional conversation in context would help the students become more aware of their uses of strategies and give them meaningful feedback about what proficient readers and writers do.

To enhance strategic and reflective thinking, they decided to use a list of reflective questions as a framework for helping them all become more astute process observers. The questions were organized around intent, engagement, and artifact, categories they had read about in a book they read together, *Creating Curriculum* (Short & Burke, 1991). At the intent level, the students were able to discuss what they were doing without much difficulty. Questions about why something was important to them were not too difficult to highlight. The teachers consciously demonstrated the idea of intent as they talked about why they were doing certain things and why they were important, and expected the students to be able to do this as well.

Explanations at the artifact stage were more familiar to the students than engagement, because they had practice explaining why various pieces of work had been selected for their portfolios. Their comments about their learning at the end of an experience were fairly superficial ("I did a good job. I worked hard."). However, the teachers felt they could improve the reflections; through demonstration and conferencing, they could all learn how to be more insightful.

The engagement stage seemed to be the most difficult. So much talk was going on all the time, it was hard to notice the cues the students were paying attention to as they made decisions about their learning. It seemed that while the students were involved in learning experiences, there was too much going on to pay attention to the students' individual thinking processes. It would be necessary for the students to be more aware and reflective of what they were doing and to make notes about it, as a way of helping the teachers understand what was happening when they weren't directly involved or available.

Mary called the class together to discuss self-evaluation and how to keep notes about their learning. Early in the discussion, she asked the class how they knew they were learning. Some of the children said they knew because the teachers told them they had done a good job, complimented them, or had given them a good grade. The idea of recognizing, which they had learned through expanded personal awareness of their own processes, was not yet in place for most of the students. The prevailing belief was that evaluation was beyond their control and was the teachers' responsibility, not theirs. Evaluation was something done *to* them, not *by* them.

To make the idea of self-awareness more concrete, Mary and Penny asked the class what they would do when they had enough to eat (stop eating), were tired of playing (stop playing), or wanted to find out about something (read a book). Then they asked how they would know they were full, tired, or curious. This was harder, as the conversation turned to specific indicators tied to one condition or another. It was talk time well spent, however. When the discussion returned to the immediate issue of knowing that they were learning and how to keep track of it, they saw the connections and began to identify their own learning behaviors.

Anecdotal observations were a critical part of documenting the learning. A literacy checklist used in the district was a good guide. The teachers also paid attention to the development of interpersonal skills and looked for instances of collaboration, risk taking, and reflective talk. They struggled with managing a record-keeping system, and Penny developed a process checklist that helped track observations as they occurred. However, it was easy for them to become involved in the group process and forget to record what was going on. It soon occurred to them that they were not the only evaluators and observers in the classroom, and needed to enlist the students' help. If the students were to be aware of their learning and become articulate about their process, they had to be intimately involved, every step of the way.

One simple change was to encourage the students to participate in the anecdotal recording system. Mary kept an index card for each student on a clipboard for note taking about their learning. She made entries on a regular basis, noting instances of risk taking, collaborating, questioning, reflecting, and the use of strategies. Mary made her notes available to the students and encouraged them to add their comments to hers. They enjoyed taking some ownership in this, and the record keeping became less of a burden.

10/2 great prediction!
      yes!

10/5 you did a great job figuring out the word "pretended" - I can tell you were really thinking ☺
      I swondend it out and loooked at the word to coorect it. Then it mad sens.

10/2 You were right! Helen did learn to talk - good predicting. I think Ann Sullivin will stay!

10/4 Steven, I like the way you're thinking when you're reading - good job!
      Yes when I don't get it I read it agen.

Journaling also took on new meaning when students were encouraged to stop frequently during their work and write down what they noticed themselves doing, thinking, and learning. There was renewed interest in literature response journals, which had become routine and boring. Now they were vehicles for recording the key points of group discussions with interpretations about the questions asked, comments made, and issues raised. The student motivation came from knowing they would be sharing these journals with the teachers and that they were helping keep track of what everyone was doing.

When interest groups were started in first grade, everything the students did was celebrated. Anything and everything was encouraged, and the focus was on thinking and learning. In second grade, the focus was the same, but the students started spending too much time on the presentation and racing through the research stages. To address this concern, and to relate it to the schoolwide emphasis on quality work, Mary and her class began to talk about criteria for quality interest groups.

The class brainstormed what they felt a good interest group looked like. From the brainstorming, descriptors were listed and organized into a simple rubric, which included the process (group work), product (what was shared with the class), and presentation (the performance event). The students decided on the range of possibilities from "Not yet O.K." to "Awesome!"

The rubric was used for teacher evaluation, peer evaluation, and self-evaluation. But it only gave a limited amount of information, and the students realized they needed a place for comments so they could write more, as well as time to discuss what was going on. The students appreciated receiving peer and teacher feedback, but they got more from the comments than from any rating scale.

Video- and audiotaping were powerful tools for helping students and teachers see changes in thinking and learning that were occurring. They taped everything from literature discussions to interest group presentations. By showing these to the students and using them for reflective discussions, they became an integral part of the student evaluation process.

The students loved to be taped. They were not at all self-conscious and enjoyed watching themselves and talking about what they noticed. When the whole class watched the videotapes or listened to the audiotapes, they could ask a participant directly about what was going on.

For example, they taped Danielle as she shared her project portfolio from an interest group. Danielle was pulling out each artifact and reading her reflections aloud: "I did a good job, I picked this because it is good, I did a very good job. . . ." After a few minutes, she stopped and said, "This all sounds alike!" Danielle recognized that her comments were superficial, and capturing it on tape helped everyone see the need for thoughtful, differentiated evaluations. With Danielle as the guide, the class developed ways to make their responses reflect the quality of the content and thinking: "This writing really shows improvement. I have added lots of details." "I like this drawing because it shows what my room really looks like, kinda messy and comfortable." "This journal entry talks about another book I read that the story reminded me of."

Conferencing with individuals and small groups was ongoing and beneficial. Mary tried to meet with at least two interest groups each time they got together. She asked the students to discuss how their research was going, what was working for them, and what they needed help with. She made group notes and recorded various responses for future reference in discussions. For example, the Oprah group was having difficulty finding resources. There were only two books, so they enlisted the class to help find magazine and newspaper articles. Mary used the conference times for mediating, coaching, teaching, sharing, reflecting, and modeling problem solving.

Class meetings provided the answers to many questions. The class decided that they needed to establish a timeline for interest group completion. They also said that the presentations needed to be spread out over a week's time and that groups could sign up for presentation times; any group that did not finish could continue with their topic in a future interest group. Students took ownership of the class meeting. As a result of their participation, a stronger feeling of connectedness and caring about each other developed within the classroom community.

The students were comfortable sharing their thinking and receiving feedback from the class after various presentations; they took the idea of self evaluation and sharing evaluations very seriously. The special needs students benefited greatly from the class discussions about the tapes, and they could see and hear examples of reflective thinking that they could try to begin to internalize for themselves.

Involving Parents

Parents' Night provided the opportunity for the class to share project portfolios from interest groups as part of the larger learning portfolio. Mary's students were accustomed to talking about their work with each other. As part of the whole school preparation for portfolio night, the students had also shared their work with other classrooms of different grade levels. Mary's room shared their portfolios with the first-grade classrooms next door and across the hall. By the time Parents' Night arrived, the students were experienced in talking about their learning. They relished their family's undivided attention, and they were very articulate about their accomplishments. They explained why each piece was in the portfolio, what it represented about their learning, explained the organization of their work, and shared goals for continued learning. Parents were asked to share their thoughts with their children. Later, in a school survey, the parents' comments ranged from "positive" to "incredulous" that the children learned so much and were so articulate about the learning.

Parent-teacher conferences also reflected this student empowerment. Mary's students were participants in these conferences. The students carefully prepared to participate by organizing journals, portfolios, projects, and tapes to support and demonstrate the learning that was taking place. They explained the progress they felt they had made, and, along with their parents, set a new goal for the next quarter. Questions to lead the discussion were prepared in advance, and students practiced conferencing with each other. When the conferences began, the students took the lead, moving away from needing someone else's acknowledgment to show what they knew. When Kristen's mother asked her to show how she had improved, Kristen replied, "Oh, that's an easy one." As she spread her artifacts out, the picture was clear, but it was her commentary that made it come alive. Her reflections were thoughtful and clearly showed an awareness of process: "I chose this because it shows how I have improved. I didn't get every one right, but I came to understand how to do it." "This writing reminds me of *Amelia Bedelia*. I like to play around with words. Sometimes they can mean different things and they make me laugh!" Kristen and her mother laughed, and Mom shed a tear as they celebrated the learning that had taken place.

Three-way Conferences

Traditionally, conferences have involved only teachers and parents, with children waiting at home wondering what is being said about them. Davies, Cameron, Politano, and Gregory suggest that three-way conferences are a valuable resource. "Teachers who choose to involve their students as active participants in three-way conferencing are finding that children know a great deal about their own learning and are key informants in the reporting process" (p. 25). The teacher, parents, and student each prepare for and are involved in the discussion. Preparation guidelines suggested by the authors include self-evaluation by the student ("What am I good at?" "What do I need to improve?" "What goals have I set?"), as well as the teacher's evaluation of the student; the parents, teacher, and student also form collaborative goals for continued success in learning. They also suggest that a three-way report—rather than or in addition to the traditional report card—be sent home only *after* the conference has taken place.

Source: Davies, A., Cameron, C., Politano, C., & Gregory, K. (1992). *Taken is better: Collaborative assessment, evaluation and reporting.* Winnipeg: Peguis.

Conclusion

Interest groups came to the rescue at a time when Mary was struggling with curricular demands, district outcomes, and student ownership. The collaboration and sharing that Mary and Penny engaged in mirrored the collaboration and sharing that took place in the classroom. Through their questions and struggles came the answers to their pressing questions about interest groups—providing for student ownership and meeting district and grade level expectations. Equally important, new questions and new insights about opportunities for reflective thinking, student evaluation, and continued learning occurred as well.

> I remember my two favorite interest groups were LEGO and Chemistry. In first grade, I learned about the table of elements with Ryan and you helped us find and understand about acids and alkaline. Then, when we studied biographies in second grade, I researched Ole Christiansen, the founder of LEGO who grew up in Denmark and was a woodworker. You helped me find all the inside information. We really used our brains in interest groups. We learned so much from each other and had a good time, too. (Richard, end of year reflections)

> This type of learning is a great way to get kids to carry their lessons across many subjects. It makes learning easier and fun for everyone. School's goals should be to create and foster a love for learning. Although the methods used today are different from those used when we were in grade school, today's methods seem to create students more eager to learn and better able to reach their own individual potentials. (Richard's parents)

Reflective Commentary

From choice of topics to collaborative evaluation, the classroom environment that Mary and Penny have created glows with respect for children. Here, the overriding standard that guides classroom decisions is the commitment to treat all children as capable learners. In this classroom, students with "L.D." labels are expected to pursue personal research, children who are still getting the reading process together are given the same choice of materials as more able readers, and every child is asked to engage in reflection about the meaning and quality of his or her work. This is heady stuff, but as Penny and Mary will tell you, all of the students in this classroom experience success and grow in their perceptions of themselves as readers, writers, and independent problem-solvers.

Inclusion

Rogers (1993) uses the term "inclusion revolution" to highlight the momentum gathering in American schools to include children with disabilities in the regular classroom. She tells the story of six-year-old Joseph ("an unlikely revolutionary") who, like his older siblings, wanted to attend a Chicago magnet school. School officials, however, had a different path in mind. They felt strongly that Joe should attend a segregated school with children who had physical disabilities as he did, and argued that it was necessary so that he could receive extensive physical therapy. That isn't how his mother saw it. "She knew that no amount of physical therapy would 'cure' his cerebral palsy and that he would eventually have to earn his living using his superior intellect" (p. 1). Joe's parents struggled and protested for a full year before he was allowed to attend.

Taylor (1991) tells of a similar struggle in *Learning Denied*. Officials attempted to separate Patrick from his classmates because of a suspected disability (the mere mention of the possibility of perceptual difficulties on a preschool screening assessment). Taylor tells how Patrick's complex learning abilities were ignored while he was dehumanized and reduced to a set of test scores. Patrick's parents resisted vehemently while the school responded by increasing its efforts to label him. Patrick's struggle is a story of educators focusing only on what a student *cannot* do; Mary and Penny's is a story of helping children realize just how much they *can* do.

Inclusion refers to "the commitment to educate each child, to the maximum extent appropriate, in the school and classroom he or she would otherwise attend. It involves bringing the support services to the child (rather than moving the child to the services)" (Rogers, 1993, p. 1). Penny came to Mary's classroom during interest group time to support specifically labeled children as they were engaged in the same learning activities as the other children. Penny did not, however, single these children out in any way. She joined an interest group herself and skillfully watched for opportunities to help any child who needed her.

Inquiry-Based Evaluation

In many child- and meaning-centered classrooms around the country, young learners are posing questions about topics that are important to them. Within this inquiry frame, students are also asking questions about their learning processes. From inception to presentation, teachers in these classrooms ask students to monitor their work and to repeatedly ask themselves and others, "How's it going? What successful strategies am I using? Which ones should I modify? What am I learning from this experience?" This process is termed inquiry-based evaluation (Crafton & Burke, 1994), and it involves pulling students into the evaluation conversation, teaching them that self-reflection is a critical and ongoing part of the larger learning cycle. "This kind of evaluation is not used for external verification, it is used for internal exploration" (p. 3).

Greer (1995) tells the story of a friend, a leader in the standards movement, who jokingly said, "Our motto is Standards: We set 'em, you keep 'em" (p. 27). Greer suggests that we want more from standard setting than a simple "write them, print them, keep them." She shares how two groups of students involved in writers' circles have learned to focus on very different things. One group asks questions that focus on trivial and superficial aspects of the writing (e.g., "Did you know you erased so hard that you made a hole in the paper?" "Is that the right way to spell this?"). The other group "split their attention between a piece of student writing and a rubric that was posted on the wall. The rubric spelled out the important features of various genres in which students might be writing (e.g., uses supporting detail, uses describing words, uses dialogue, uses suspense or humor to keep the reader's attention)." The second group produced qualitatively different questions (e.g., "What did you do to keep the reader's attention?" "Do you think that you have enough detail so that the reader will understand?"). Greer remarks that these are very different views of keeping standards. "Students keep forging a common language, working with shared definitions of quality, and using those standards to shape and revise their own work and the work of their peers" (p. 27).

In one publication, rubrics are defined as "a set of scoring guidelines for evaluating student work. The rubric answers the question: What does mastery (and varying degrees of mastery) at a task look like?" (The Center on Learning, Assessment, and School Structure, 1994, p. 1). In contrast, Penny and Mary engaged in rubric development *with* the students. Collaborative efforts such as this help everyone understand what constitutes quality work. The essence of collaborative and inquiry-based evaluation is the conversation regarding dimensions of quality. Learners, then, must crawl inside an experience and consider its dimensions and the outcomes of various decisions *on an ongoing basis,* throughout the learning process. It is the *act* of questioning and thinking and talking—the act of generating the rubric, guideline, or standard—that makes the learning difference. Once the rubric has been produced, though, it must be written in pencil, constantly inviting change and rethinking. The talk cannot be about high standards that have already been identified, but of those still being invented (Wolf & Pistone, 1991).

The Structure of Learning

Mary wanted to move from first grade to second grade with her students, but one question everyone needed to reflect on was how to make her second-grade curriculum different from her first-grade curriculum.

Americans are accustomed to grade-level designations for their children; "What grade are you in?" is an almost inevitable question people tend to ask children. The real questions are, however, whether grade levels are the most beneficial way to structure learning and whether learning should change from one grade level to the next when students are placed in these designations.

Organizing schools by grades assumes that students of certain ages should achieve certain objectives and master particular skills. Language and literacy learning, though, are about the development of underlying processes and strategies, not the mastery of an arbitrary set of objectives from one age or grade to the next.

Harste (1993) discusses old curricular anchors and argues for a new perspective for language arts learning and instruction:

> One of these (old) anchors was the belief that there is an inherent order to learning language and that this order could be used as a basis for sequencing instruction. This anchor undergirded a skills-based approach to the teaching of reading and the language arts. Another anchor was the belief that there is an inherent order in mental development and that this order could be used to plan appropriate instruction. This anchor was the argument undergirding a developmental perspective on curriculum.
>
> Inquiry into what young children know about reading and writing prior to going to school seriously challenged these curricular anchors. From what researchers could tell there is no inherent order in language and the way it is learned, nor is there a developmental sequence that children go through in their attempt to learn language (Donaldson, 1978; Harste, Woodward, & Burke, 1984). The young mind seems ready to learn lots of things. Some five year olds, for example, know as much, if not more, about stories and storiness as do some sixth graders. The key to understanding language learning is *experience* . . . not age, stage, or Piaget.

Penny describes grade-level designations as an "adult management tool." Baker, Aulgur, and Copeland concur: "The system did not start out placing children in self-contained grade levels, but because of increasing school enrollments and the economics of organizing large numbers of children in one building, students were divided according to age. If all learners had similar background knowledge and experiences, had the same interests, and learned at the same pace, this kind of arrangement would work. This, however, is *not* the case" (1992, p. 1).

Mary's focus, then, on continuing to nurture her students' researching and problem-solving abilities was exactly right—these are lifelong learning needs that can only be strengthened through ongoing meaningful experience. These are process-based engagements that cannot stop after one or two brief encounters; they must follow students through the primary grades into the intermediate grades, middle school, and high school, because they will surely follow them after that and for the rest of their lives.

What Key Standards Emerge and Interact in This Context?

Students read a range of print and nonprint texts. Interest groups explored a range of materials to gather information for their inquiry: newspapers, TV, magazines, reference books, nonfiction, and biographies. Members of the Helen Keller interest group learned some sign language and parts of the Braille alphabet. Members of the country music group explored music and dance along with textual material.

Students apply a range of strategies. One interest group wrote letters to a hearing-impaired class that included pictures, information about themselves, and questions about how they could "talk" through signing. Students watched and discussed a video from the hearing impaired group in which they signed greetings, the alphabet, and something about themselves.

Students adapt conventions to communicate effectively. Reflective discussions, videos, and audiotapes helped students in Mary's classroom develop a sensitivity to audience, language choice, and clarity of presentation (including content, pace, voice level, enunciation). They viewed and compared their "performances" in literature discussions, interest group presentations, and portfolio sharing. The interest group presentations gave them opportunity to examine different presentation formats like talk shows, videos, charts, graphs, and timelines.

Students use knowledge of language structure, language conventions, media techniques, and genre. One group of students created a videotape to send to another classroom. During their reading of biographies, all groups discussed the structure of the genre and made judgments about the quality of individual works. As they prepared final presentations of their research, groups discussed, drafted, and edited content.

Students research issues and interests. All students belonged to groups that researched famous people they had chosen. The umbrella theme was biographies so this genre was highlighted as a major resource. All groups identified questions, planned their inquiry, investigated their topic using multiple resources (one group interviewed and exchanged videos with another group of students to help them understand what it means to be deaf and how the deaf communicate), and shared their knowledge in different ways (e.g., portfolios, talk shows, timelines, pictorial collage).

Students use technological and information resources. Students used videotapes and audiotapes to evaluate their learning. They taped everything from literature discussions to interest group presentations so that they might engage in reflective discussions about content and process and set future goals for similar engagements. One interest group created a videotape to send to a hearing-impaired classroom—and received one in return, resulting in a multimedia correspondence which pushed both groups to think through how to use video technology to develop a relationship and to represent certain parts of themselves.

Students participate in a variety of literacy communities. Students belonged to and participated in a number of literacy communities: the larger classroom group—reading, writing, and evaluating together—their specific interest group, those readers who explore biographies, people who understand and can use some sign language. Within these communities, students posed questions, researched interests, reported their knowledge, created a video, and engaged in long-term and intensive evaluation of the processes and products of their learning (e.g., portfolios were created for their biography projects and the accompanying reflections were videotaped for group and individual analysis; students made observations of themselves and others collaborating, questioning, and taking risks, and added these observations to Mary's anecdotal notes; literature discussions were taped and critiqued so that students could set future goals for changing the quality of their discussions). Perhaps the most impressive thinking displayed in the interest groups was related to the reflections about the roles and accomplishments of women in our society—a result of inquiry into the lives of Oprah Winfrey and Helen Keller. The students' discussions showed that their perceptions about people with physical handicaps and women in general had changed.

Students use spoken, written, and visual language to accomplish their own purposes. Students in Mary's classroom often discussed the independent inquiry they were engaged in outside of the classroom. Some students engaged in and shared focused inquiry when they were on vacation.

References and Other Resources

Adler, D. (1990). *A picture book of Helen Keller.* New York: Penguin.

Baker, L., Aulgur, L., & Copeland, K. (1992). Multiage classrooms: Option to an outdated system. *Teachers Networking, 11*(2), 1–4.

Barnes, D. (1995). Talking and learning in classrooms: An introduction. *Primary Voices K–6, 3*(1), 2–7.

Copenhaver, J. (1992). Instances of inquiry. *Primary Voices K–6*, Premier Issue, 6–14.

Crafton, L. (1991). *Whole language: Getting started . . . moving forward.* Katonah, NY: Richard C. Owen.

Crafton, L., & Burke, C. (1994). Inquiry-based evaluation: Teachers and students reflecting together. *Primary Voices K–6, 2*(2), 2–7.

Donaldson, M. (1978). *Children's minds.* Glasgow: William Collins.

Greer, E. A. (1995). Standards: A new language for expectation and equity. *Voices from the Middle, 2*(1), 27–28.

Harste, J. C. (1993). Library as curricular conversations about knowledge, inquiry, and morality. In M. Ruddell and R. Ruddell (Eds.), *Theoretical models and processes of reading* (4th ed.).

Harste, J. C., Woodward, V. A., & Burke, C. L. (1984). *Language stories and literacy lessons.* Portsmouth, NH: Heinemann.

Hill, B. C., Johnson, N. J., & Schlick Noe, K. L. (1995). *Literature circles and response.* Norwood, MA: Christopher-Gordon.

Kasten, W. (1993). *The multiage classroom: A family of learners.* Katonah, NY: Richard C. Owen.

Pierce, K. M., & Gilles, C. (1994). *Cycles of meaning.* Portsmouth, NH: Heinemann.

Rogers, J. (1993). The inclusion revolution. *Research Bulletin,* Phi Delta Kappa, p. 11.

Short, K., & Burke, C. (1991). *Creating curriculum.* Portsmouth, NH: Heinemann.

Silvers, P. (1994). Everyday signs of learning. *Primary Voices K–6, 2*(2), 20–31.

Taylor, D. (1990). *Learning denied.* Portsmouth, NH: Heinemann.

Von Dras, J. (1995). Will the real teacher please stand up? *Primary Voices K–6, 3*(1), 30–38.

Wolf, D. P., & Pistone, N. (1991). *Taking full measure: Rethinking assessment through the arts.* New York: College Entrance Examination Board.

CHAPTER SIX

INQUIRY AND THE IDITAROD

Before reading, consider . . .
- *One topic you would love to learn more about.*
- *What resources would you need to enable you to learn?*
- *What conditions would best facilitate your learning?*
- *What topics the children in your classroom have a passion for.*

For three days the children had listened to the story of Willy, a ten-year-old boy determined to keep the farm going and to give his ailing grandfather a reason to live. For three days they held their breath as Willy and his dog Searchlight tried to outrun the best dogsled racers in the country, including the legendary Shoshone Indian, Stone Fox. And, finally, they sat spellbound as their teacher read the end of the race:

> The crowd cheered madly when they saw little Willy come into view at the far end of Main Street, and even more madly when they saw that Stone Fox was right on his tail.
> "Go, Searchlight! Go!"
> Searchlight gave it everything she had. She was a hundred feet from the finish line when her heart burst. She died instantly. There was no suffering. (Gardiner, *Stone Fox*, p. 77)

There was stunned silence in the classroom. Not one of the twenty-three suburban second graders moved. Finally, a collective sigh, and then the responses and the questions:

> "Why did the puppy have to die?"
> "The author could have let her live, couldn't he?"
> "This is the worst book we've ever read."
> "How much did the sled weigh? It was just too heavy for her—Willy shouldn't have let her race."
> "The race was too long and hard for her—Stone Fox's dogs were bigger—they could handle it."
> "I thought it was going to be a happy ending."
> "If I had been Willy, I would have found another way to raise the money."

"Are there real races like that? Probably the people running them wouldn't let a little dog like Searchlight into the race, would they?"

Marcia Sostrin, a veteran teacher, encouraged the talk. She knew the emotions would run high with this book and that many of the children would feel Searchlight's death deeply because of their love for their own dogs. Marcia had given her students many opportunities to respond to literature over the past few months. Throughout the year they had kept literature logs and engaged in literature discussions. These developing readers had learned to expand their responses to books and stories by relating material to their own experiences and by exchanging interpretations. Now, the responses swelled and filled the classroom; after they lost their edge, the explosion was replaced with quiet reflection. A half-raised hand indicated another question: "Are there *real* dogsled races like the one in the book?"

Marcia had carefully selected *Stone Fox* for two reasons. First, she loved the book and knew it would elicit a strong discussion. She also knew it had the potential to lead them into a new area of inquiry. It was only a few weeks until the Iditarod, Alaska's annual 1,000-mile dogsled race. She described the race briefly and told the children she had a film, "Beyond Courage," that she wanted them to see. They watched the mushers prepare for the race, felt the strength and energy of the huskies speeding through the snow, and celebrated with the winner as she crossed the finish line in Nome. Now they had more questions, and there seemed little doubt that this was how Marcia and her students would spend much of their time during the next month.

Through discussions with a local teacher educator whose daughter was in her class, Marcia had been thinking about the idea of perspective in learning. She was convinced that one effective way to achieve more authentic content integration was to encourage her students to ask questions and then, based on those curiosities, explore the topic from multiple perspectives. Marcia decided to ask her students to begin their inquiry by brainstorming a list of questions they had about the race:

- Exactly how long is it?
- What do the dogs eat?
- Do they sleep?
- Do they train for the race like the Olympics?
- Do the dogs ever get hurt?
- Are there many women who do the Iditarod?
- How long has the Iditarod been running?
- Do the dogs have to try out?
- Are the dogs pets?
- Do they win prizes?
- Do they have helpers on the sleds?
- What if there's a snow storm?

She then asked if they thought there were certain groups of people involved in the race who might share similar questions. "The sled drivers." "Doctors." "People who live there." "TV people." "News reporters." Slowly, a perspective list was made:

- The Mushers
- Veterinarians

When Reading Materials Are Too Difficult: Professional Resources

Allington, R. L. (1983). The reading instruction provided readers of differing reading abilities. *The Elementary School Journal, 83,* 548–559.

Copperman, P. (1986). *Taking books to heart: How to develop a love of reading in your child.* Reading, MA: Addison-Wesley.

Crafton, L. K. (1983). Learning from reading: What happens when students generate their own background information. *Journal of Reading, 26.*

Fielding, L., & Roller, C. (1992). Making difficult books accessible and easy books acceptable. *The Reading Teacher, 45,* 678–685.

Labbo, L., & Teale, W. H. (1990). Cross-age reading: A strategy for helping poor readers. *The Reading Teacher, 43,* 364–369.

Rhodes, L., & Dudley-Marling, K. (1990). *Readers and writers with a difference.* Portsmouth, NH: Heinemann.

Stephens, D. (1990). *What matters: A primer for teaching reading.* Portsmouth, NH: Heinemann.

Watson, D. J., Burke, C., & Harste, J. (1989). *Whole language: Inquiring voices.* Ontario: Scholastic.

- Anchorage Residents
- Newspaper Reporters
- Animal Lovers

Because Marcia wanted to expand their perspectives, she suggested that they add one more:

- Historians

Marcia passed out a question book with a perspective listed on each page. The second graders took their journals home for two nights and, along with their parents, brainstormed questions once again. Afterwards, they considered which of the questions might be asked from which perspectives, and those were listed on the appropriate pages.

When the journals came back to school, Marcia led a discussion about which perspectives were easy to generate questions for and which ones were hard. Why would that be true? Did moms and dads have trouble with any of the perspectives? And which were their favorites, and why? Marcia put a special emphasis on the questions. Were any of them particularly important to them? Did they feel strongly about or personally connected to any questions? Why? Now they were ready to choose their three favorite perspectives. These were written down so Marcia could make an effort to give everyone their first or second choice.

The weekend the race started, the students were encouraged to watch it on TV. On Monday, the real excitement began. Marcia had learned from a parent that there was a toll-free number they could call each day for an update on the race. So, every morning, there was great speculation about who was in the lead (the girls always rooted for Susan Butcher, a musher who had won the race several times before). Jessica had volunteered to draw a large map with all of the checkpoints marked so a miniature husky could be moved along and pinned to the most current one.

Each afternoon the students gathered in their perspective groups for an hour to organize and to research using the materials Marcia had gathered. In addition, some unexpected resources surfaced. Samantha's mom had a friend teaching in Alaska, and a phone call to her elicited a promise to send local newspaper articles each day. Joey's grandparents were friends with Martin Buser, one of the best-known mushers; they had pictures of his home and training area, and could possibly arrange a phone interview. Another teacher in the school knew a local person who raised huskies, and he was available to speak to the class. An on-line computer service carried news of the race every day.

From the first day of the group gatherings, it was clear that reading was going to be a problem; many of the books available on the Iditarod had information that several groups needed at the same time, and many of the print materials were too difficult for a significant number of students in the class. The problem of too few texts and too many readers was presented to the class.

What solutions could they think of? Once more, a brainstormed list produced a number of alternatives. They settled on drawing numbers to see which group would get a certain book first and how the books would get circulated among the groups.

Marcia had dealt with the difficult texts problem many times before and had never let that issue prevent her students from pursuing questions they were dying to know the answers to. She settled on four strategies. First, she read aloud from the on-line copy each day while students followed along on their individual sheets. Each student had a highlighter to mark segments that might be helpful to the perspective groups. Later, they went back to those marked sections to reread and discuss. Second, she sometimes paired readers with more experienced peers or older students. They engaged in a version of shared reading in which the less experienced reader identified the parts she or he wanted to read, and the other parts were read by the partner. Third, she taught her students to use reader-selected miscues. When they were read-

Reader-Selected Miscues
Dorothy J. Watson

Why?

1. To put the reader in control of the reading task, so that the reader and the author are allowed their own transaction without interruptions from outsiders;
2. To show students that everyone, even proficient readers, makes miscues;
3. To demonstrate to students that some miscues move the reader right along in the text while others disrupt meaning;
4. To provide the teacher with trustworthy information about a student's reading.

How?

Before silent reading time, give each student several 2" × 8" bookmarks. Ask the students to read as usual but to stop momentarily when they encounter any difficulty in reading. They are to place a bookmark at the trouble spot, and then continue reading.

A few minutes before the end of the reading time, ask the students to examine their miscues and to select three that caused problems in the long run of the reading, that is, miscues that caused them to lose the meaning of the text or to be distracted from the reading. Ask the students to write on each bookmark one of the sentences that contained a miscue and to underline the problem. They add their names to the bookmarks as well.

Collect the bookmarks and categorize the miscues. Study the miscues carefully to determine the cause of the problem, such as overuse of phonics, lack of concepts, difficulties with grammar, making inferences, etc.

Children can be grouped together to briefly discuss the problems they have encountered. Discussions should center around alternate ways (strategies) to solve the problem with an invitation to notice when it comes up again so individuals can share their strategies with the group or whole class.

(This description varies slightly from the original, which appears in Watson, D. J. (Ed.). (1987). *Ideas and insights: Language arts in the elementary school.* Urbana, IL: National Council of Teachers of English.

ing silently, they were asked to keep a blank bookmark handy on which to record difficult words or sections of text. Later, she met with them to discuss a few selected problems. This strategy was used by all students, so no one was singled out as a problem reader. Finally, she taught them all to use a scanning strategy. Reading strategies such as predicting, confirming, and rereading had been discussed repeatedly during the year. Now the second graders added scanning to find key words and specific information. This resulted in groups supporting each other's inquiries as much as their own: "Hey, Animal Lovers! We found something in this book you just *have* to read."

Marcia wanted her students to become aware of the many ways they were gathering information and constructing knowledge; she was as interested in helping them understand their research process as she was in getting answers to their questions. Each group created a reflective journal, in which they recorded the strategies they used each day. During the last five minutes of research time, they were asked to think about *how* they learned new information as they focused on and researched individual questions.

Other strategies the groups identified included interviewing, talking, reading (brochures, newspapers, books, articles, maps, charts, and lists), comparing facts, asking an expert, and doing surveys. One day Marcia teamed the groups and asked them to talk about how the research was going and what strategies were working best. Then, she pulled them together for a whole-class discussion on how different ways of gathering information are more or less effective, depending on the questions you are asking.

Marcia knew that she also needed a way to keep track of what the children were doing. She found that looking through her professional journals helped focus her observations in three areas that she believed were important: process, attitude, and sharing knowledge.

She showed this form to her students so they would know what she thought was most important. After the study, she hoped to revise it by having conversations with her students about what *they* thought was central to the research.

Each day she spent the inquiry hour doing three things: sharing materials with specific groups, roaming the room to troubleshoot (answering reading questions, making suggestions when asked to help solve a negative group interaction, gently reminding the students that all members need to be involved), and making anecdotal notes for one targeted group.

This was a great study. It was filled with daily cheers, focused investigation, and a classroom whirling with new knowledge. Suddenly, though, there was a dark cloud. One afternoon, one of the groups stopped their work and called for everyone's attention. They had made a terrible discovery: the huskies, raised in the outback of Alaska specifically to run the Iditarod, had to be the best and the strongest, and if they weren't, they were killed. Once again, stunned silence. But this time the silence was followed by anger and outrage, and Marcia wondered how she could now sanction the study of this topic. Marcia had gone to her class with an invitation to study the Iditarod with full knowledge of the past controversies regarding the health of the dogs during the race. She knew that in the past the huskies had sometimes suffered frostbite and exhaustion from being pushed too hard, but she had also been convinced that these problems had been successfully addressed through the efforts of animal rights activists—in fact, the Animal Rights Perspective Group was researching that very thing. This, however, cast a shadow on the students' excitement.

Marcia did a slow turn, making eye contact with every child. In a low, even tone that captured the responsibility inherent in her question, she said, "What should we do?" The children looked uncomfortably at each other, and those standing shifted their weight from one foot to the other. They seemed to be wrestling with the enormity of the question, believing, as Marcia did, that they had to do something.

Teri called out the first suggestion: "Remember when we studied the rain forest and collected money and wrote letters? Maybe we could do that again."

"I don't think that's enough! Maybe we could adopt the puppies that aren't strong enough so they won't be killed."

"But how could we do that? Who would keep them and how would we get them here? And, anyway, probably the mushers wouldn't even tell anyone if they had a weak puppy."

Marcia reminded them that they had the address for the Iditarod Headquarters, and suggested that they might want to start with that and perhaps to also contact the magazine that reported the atrocity to find out where they got their information. It was decided that two people would write to the magazine while others would draft a letter to send to the organizing committee, and everyone would sign it. The next morning, several students brought in individual letters protesting the killing practice. These were included with the whole class letter. They mailed these off and waited.

From that moment on, the inquiry shifted. While everyone continued to meet in their perspective groups to continue their research, much of the discussion and reading became focused on the huskies running the race and the ones left behind in the outback. What more could they find out about the dogs? What more could they do?

One day Kevin came in and said he had heard that in some places, it wasn't only weak animals that were killed, but sometimes baby girls were, too. There were gasps. "Not true." "It couldn't be true . . . is it, Mrs. Sostrin?" Yes, in some countries, it was. Another injustice—they would talk to the librarian and see what they could find out. Should they raise more money and write more letters?

Now the conversations turned to other social injustices, particularly homelessness. Samantha said that she was going to the public library on Saturday to

March 17, 1994

Dear Iditarod Trail Committee,

Our 2nd grade class has been researching the Iditarod. We read an article that said some of the dogs are killed just because they are not strong enough to race in the Iditarod.

We think it's wrong to kill the dogs. They are living beings and they are perfectly good dogs. They could be pets or sent to a pet store. We think that anyone who kills a dog should be disqualified from the race.

Maybe your committee could set up an adopt-a-Husky program.

Please write back to us.

Sincerely,

Mrs. Sostrin's
2nd Grade Class
Wilmot Elementary
Deerfield, IL 60015

Dear Iditarod Trail Committee,
I read an article about how mushers kill dogs. They only let live 24 dogs. But I have an opinion. Any mushers who kill the dogs because their not strong should be disqualified! Because that dogs thinks hes about to see the world. But then he dies and doesn't get to see the world. If every mushers kills Huskies. They'll be on the enlarged specier list. Stop this killing while you can.

Sincerely,
Katie Speth
Katie Speth

STOP KILLING THE HUSKIES!!!!!!!!!

huskie!!!

THE HUSKIES ARE OUR FRIENDS!!!!!!!!!

hear Michael Rosen, an author who had written a book for the homeless. He was donating all of his profits to benefit the homeless. Samantha suggested that everyone go and buy his books—maybe they could study about the homeless after the Iditarod was over. Marcia began to mentally plan for their next inquiry.

Marcia decided that this was a good time to have the local husky owner come in and talk about raising these dogs, and to specifically ask his opinion on what they had read about the weaker dogs being killed. The owner shared specifics about caring for huskies and showed slides from a trip to Alaska. When asked about the article, he highlighted the loving relationship that owners have with their dogs and said he was sure that was true with the mushers in Alaska—in fact, he knew that a loving bond between musher and team was a critical point for anyone who wanted to win the race, because they had to trust each other and work as a well-oiled unit. Wouldn't this kind of love extend to all the musher's dogs, even the ones who weren't strong enough to run in the race? Could the article have been some kind of propaganda to convince people not to support the Iditarod?

"You mean you think it might not be true?" Amy's voice carried the surprise felt by everyone in the classroom. Here was a whole new take on the issue, and Marcia recognized the teaching gift she had just been handed—an unexpected opportunity to expand the idea of perspective and critical reading.

The next day she used the magazine article as a starting point to encourage her students to think about the idea of "truth" in writing. When someone has a particular purpose for writing, is the piece likely to present the whole truth and all sides of the issue? What about the personal experience stories they had been writing? What if someone else—mom, dad, a brother, a sister, a friend—involved in the experience had written the story? Would it be the same? Not long after this discussion, the second graders received a response to the letter they had written protesting the puppy killings. It, too, suggested that the alarming statement the children had found was some form of propaganda. The letter also reinforced the local husky owner's statements about the loving relationships that must exist between the mushers and dogs. This time the children needed no prompting to take a critical look at the committee's response. Could *this* also be propaganda? What reasons could they have for writing a letter like this? What's important to the people on this committee?

Shortly after Marcia's second graders scrutinized the letter, the first Iditarod musher and his weary dogs crossed the finish line. The Iditarod ended with much celebration, in Nome, Alaska, and in Marcia's second-grade classroom. During the final days of the race, the groups had begun to talk about how they would share what they had learned. Once again, they brainstormed a list of possibilities: plays, reports, posters, videotapes, question/answer books, drawings, charts, graphs, and games. Marcia sent a letter home to parents, asking if they could help the groups find time outside of school to work on their presentations. She also asked them to come on the day of the celebration to get a first-hand look at the work that had consumed their children for so many weeks. Groups volunteered to write to the principal and the curriculum coordinator to invite them to see the results of their inquiry.

Creating the presentations turned out to be one of the rockiest parts of the inquiry, especially for the two groups that had decided to develop videotapes. While the second-graders were accustomed to first and final drafts in writing, the idea didn't quite translate into video, where all revisions have to be made *before* and not during the taping. A cycle of writing, taping, rewriting, and retaping left these groups (parents included) feeling frustrated and pressured with the celebration deadline. Marcia realized that even this part of the inquiry requires conversation about process and procedure to help it go more smoothly.

As parents and administrators poured into Marcia's classroom, she handed them a program announcing the perspective groups and how they would share their research. A few pages at the back contained the children's final reflections on the Iditarod study:

> The best part was finding out that I could read really hard books—with only a little help.

> I told my mom and dad that we were doing a very important thing when we wrote the letter about the puppies being killed.

> I liked reading all those books and magazines and finding out about the racers and how they take care of their dogs.

> My group worked really well together. Like sometimes I would think of an important problem and tell my group and we would do it together. And sometimes other people would think of the problem and then I would ask myself: "Is this *really* important?" Now I'm asking myself that when we do math problems in our book.

Reflective Commentary

Deep within Marcia Sostrin's teaching is a set of values that guide her instruction and focus her observations. She thinks of these values as a list of "musts" when she is creating a learning experience for her students:

- The learning *must* be child-centered, taking into account her students' interests, questions, and curiosities.
- The learning *must* include time for reading, writing, interaction, and reflection.

- She *must* assume multiple roles to make the learning work; sometimes teaching directly, other times gathering resources, most of the time watching closely to see how she can support what the students are doing.

This set of personal guidelines has been evolving during her many years as an educator. Lately, a new issue has been swirling beneath the surface of her teaching, slowly taking shape and vying for space on her coveted list of "musts." This issue is related to the differences she sees in her students, primarily the diverse perspectives they take on the world, and also how each of them embraces their own set of values that influence how they interpret what they read and how they present their ideas in writing.

Murray says that as educators, we should be seeking diversity, not proficient mediocrity. This idea takes on enormous dimensions in the face of our challenge to implement "standards." How is it possible to deal with a series of statements about what all students should do and know, and still honor the individual faces surrounding us every day in the classroom—a "standard" that every teacher has to somehow bring to life? Teachers like Marcia show us one way to solve the equal, yet different tension. Schools that strive to promote similar thinking abilities for all students while honoring their diversity *must* encourage students to generate their own questions while always remaining open to a shift in personal interests.

Marcia had a learning framework in mind when she approached her students. She wanted to encourage multiple perspectives on the topic; she wanted a wide range of resources to answer their questions; she wanted them to explore ideas collaboratively through reading, writing, and talk; and she wanted them to be responsible for sharing their information. She had already done a great deal of "planning to plan" before she read one riveting page of *Stone Fox*, a book she had carefully selected because she knew it would touch their hearts and possibly open their minds.

"Planning to plan" (Watson, Burke, & Harste, 1989) refers to the initial decisions a teacher makes before students are intimately involved in an inquiry. The tentative nature of the term is the key. Whole learning experiences cannot be planned in detail before students get involved. Learners must be integral contributors to the decision-making process, not passive sideliners waiting to implement someone else's best-laid plans. However, sketching a flexible frame will give teachers an opportunity to support from the beginning while keeping a watchful eye for the directions students may need to take. Planning to plan forms the basis for deciding what gets explored, the strategies appropriate to the investigation, and the resources that need to be tracked down. Planning to plan gives us the impetus to replace teacher-made units with the beauty of creating with our students. It also reminds us that good teaching is opportunistic; our greatest chance of influencing all of our students comes when we remain open to incidental happenings and genuine concerns.

Marcia chose literature as a starting point for planning, but an inquiry cycle can begin anywhere—a current event, a content topic, a student, or a teacher's interest. Once a point of departure is established, everyone brainstorms the questions they have and possible strategies for answering those questions. What materials would be useful? How about other resources besides print materials?

Is there a way to weave in technology? Are there any classroom experts or parent experts? What about videotapes and audiotapes? Eventually, groups need a plan of action to decide how they will start and how responsibilities will be shared and carried out. Often, action plans are most effective when they are created each time a group meets for extended work.

The first year Marcia and her students studied the Iditarod, she felt rushed and knew her students did, too. She knew that more time before and after the race could make all the difference in depth of engagement and the development of research abilities. Hopeful that her next class would be as enthusiastic as this one, she started to plan for the February kick-off in September:

> I knew I needed to set aside a month for this research if my students wanted to do it. So I took a long, hard look at the rest of my curriculum. I had to make some tough choices, but in the end, it made for better quality teaching and learning all the way around. The second grade is required to cover certain content units throughout the year, and I decided I could condense many of these and still maintain a high level of learning. Many units have pages and pages of activities—I had to be selective about choosing the most meaningful and challenging ones. Then I was careful to integrate as much as I could, so much of what we teach can be connected, we just have to look for the ties.
>
> When February rolled around, not only did I feel that my teaching until then was more effective than ever, but I had the month I wanted to immerse my students in this exciting study.
>
> The Iditarod didn't stop when the race was over. Now that my students had the idea of perspective, we used it to study China and the panda bears, which is a required topic. They did many comparisons of this unit with Alaska and the Iditarod, so I felt that the next topics were greatly enriched because we had taken the time to do an in-depth study that the students were really excited about.

Marcia left room in her plans for her students and the inevitable surprises that surface when people follow their interests. Marcia knew that the idea of alternative perspectives could begin to encourage her students to see the world in a new way, but how could she have anticipated the level of critical thought that was fostered when her students suddenly encountered a real atrocity?

The world is filled with atrocities—and with writing (like the puppy-killing article and the Iditarod Committee's letter) meant to convince us to abandon one set of values and replace them with another. Inquiry studies consistently yield a flood of real-world materials and experiences that only need to be acted upon to develop what Brell calls the "critical spirit" (1990, p. 87).

The authors of the English language arts standards point repeatedly to the critical abilities that must be developed by citizens of a democracy. Barone, Eeds, & Mason (1995) argue that a reader's immersion into another world through literature often initiates inquiry, and it is through that inquiring disposition that critical thinking develops as a habit of mind. Inspired by many books, Mason shares her first-grade students' growing curiosities, something she encourages throughout the curriculum.

It seems that, as teachers, we cannot only be concerned about knowledge and transmitting strategic skills. Rather, we must also strive to engender a critical disposition. Emily, a second-grader in Mason's classroom, puts it this way:

full of quetions

I am raining with quetios. I do not no why. How do eggs hach? How do rainbows from? Why do bees sting? I am raining with quetions.

By, Emily

What Key Standards Emerge and Interact in This Context?

Students read a range of print and nonprint texts. Students read a wide range of materials during their Iditarod inquiry: magazines, books on the race, books on Alaska, newspapers, brochures, training guidelines. They also viewed videotapes related to the race and Alaska. They listened to a husky trainer talk about how the dogs are raised and the relationship between dog and owner. They gathered specific information from these texts depending on the perspective they were taking. Students created maps and diagrams of the race. They took alternate perspectives on the Iditarod Committee's letter and on the magazine article reporting the puppy killings: What are the reasons these documents were produced? Who wrote them? And why? They presented their knowledge to peer and adult audiences during the celebration.

Students apply a range of strategies. Students explored feelings and values in relation to different materials that evoked a strong personal reaction. They learned to take a critical stance in relation to written material by asking specific questions about the intent and perspective of the author(s). They used the idea of perspective to help them select and present various kinds of information about the Iditarod. Students used scanning in their search for specific information to help answer their research questions. They learned strategies for dealing with difficult text such as the R.S.V.P. procedure.

Students adapt conventions to communicate effectively. Students varied their organization and voice as they wrote reports, letters, and video scripts during the Iditarod inquiry. They discussed the differences in the presentation formats and how the language they chose, diagrams, illustrations, use of music, and costume needed to be taken into consideration as they communicated their content in various forms.

Students in inquiry groups took and shared notes with one another as they gathered information related to their perspective. There were ongoing discussions of how to locate specific information in books, magazines, and online computer databases, and then transfer that into research journals. Information that was gathered in one form was then used as a basis for thinking through and organizing final presentations. Inquiry groups chose a variety of ways to communicate what they had learned: videos, news reports, charts, graphs, question/answer books, and so on. Students explored different ways of talking as they planned and implemented their inquiry, requested resources, reflected on their progress and use of strategies, and made formal presentations to peers, teacher, administrators, and parents.

Students use knowledge of language structure, language conventions, media techniques, and genre. All students engaged in writing, editing, and revising as they prepared their final inquiry presentations and when they drafted and sent the letter to the Iditarod committee. During these experiences, students responded to and critiqued one another's work, and helped each other with spelling, grammar, and larger text structure. The groups that created videotapes worked through a composition process that included scripting, taping, viewing, rewriting, revision, and consideration of how effectively a multimedia presentation communicated their most significant findings.

Students research issues and interests. Students in Marcia's classroom researched a topic of interest from different real-world perspectives. Each perspective group posed questions unique to their world view, investigated those questions by using a variety of print and nonprint resources (books, magazines, videos, photographs, newspapers, experts), discussed and selected what information was significant to their given perspective, thought critically about some information they encountered, brainstormed possible ways to present their new knowledge, and communicated their findings using a range of formats.

Students use technological and informational resources. Students viewed and selected significant information from videotapes on the Iditarod and Alaska. Two groups of students produced videotapes to communicate what they had learned. All students used an online computer service to receive updates of the race in progress and to gather current and historical information about the Iditarod.

Students participate in a variety of literacy communities. Students were involved in reading, writing, speaking, and researching activities with their classroom community and with their specific perspective groups. Leadership and support roles changed as students worked together in their collaborative inquiry. Family members were drawn into the inquiry as they brainstormed questions, watched the evening news and read newspapers with their second graders for information about the race. These students joined people around the country who passionately follow or participate in the Iditarod race every year. And through their concern and proactive stance in relation to the puppies, they also became a distant part of activist groups who monitor and press for humane reforms on behalf of the dogs who run in the Iditarod.

Students use spoken, written, and visual language to accomplish their own purposes. Long after the Iditarod inquiry, Marcia receives reports from parents and students about independent reading related to the topic, particularly consulting the newspaper for related articles. Students also continue to pose questions that were not part of the formal classroom experience.

References and Other Resources

Iditarod Resources

Cooper, M. (1988). *Racing sled dogs: An original North American sport.* New York: Clarion Books.

Crisman, R. (1983). *Racing the Iditarod trail.* New York: Dillon Press.

Dolan, E. M. (1993). *Susan Butcher and the Iditarod trail.* New York: Walker Publishing.

Dougherty, J. (1988). A legend still lives as sled dogs race across the snows. *Smithsonian,* March.

Gardiner, J. R. (1980). *Stone Fox.* New York: Harper & Row.

Gill, S. (1992). *Kiana's Iditarod.* Homer, AK: Paws IV.

O'Dell, S. (1988). *Black star, bright dawn.* Boston, MA: Houghton Mifflin.

O'Neill, C. (1988). *Dogs on duty.* Washington, DC: National Geographic Society.

Paulsen, G. (1993). *Dogteam.* New York: Delacorte Press.

Paulsen, G. (1990). *Woodsong.* New York: Puffin Books.

Reit, S. (1976). *Race against death.* New York: Scholastic.

Seibert, P. (1992). *Mush!* Brookfield, CT: Millbrook Press.

Sherwonit, B. (1991). *Iditarod–The great race to Nome.* Anchorage: Alaska Northwest Books.

Shields, M. (1991). *Can dogs talk?* Fairbanks, AK: Pyrola Publishing.

Shields, M. (1992). *Loving a happy dog.* Fairbanks, AK: Pyrola Publishing.

Standiford, N. (1989). *The bravest dog ever–The true story of Balto.* New York: Random House.

Stout, P. (1992). *Alaska women in the Iditarod.* Alaska: State Education Agency.

Contact the Iditarod Trail Committee, Inc., P.O. Box 870800, Wasilla, AK, 99687 for more resources, the film *Beyond Courage,* and a collection of teaching materials.

Children Changing the World:
Books to Support Social Responsibility

Barbour, K. (1991). *Mr. Box Tie*. San Diego, CA: Harcourt Brace.

Bunting, E. (1991). *Fly away home*. Boston: Houghton Mifflin.

Cone, M. (1992). *Come back, salmon: How a group of dedicated kids adopted Pigeon Creek and brought it back to life*. New York: Sierra Club.

DiSalvo-Ryan, D. (1991). *Uncle Willie and the soup kitchen*. New York: Morrow.

Guthrie, D. (1988). *A Rose for Abby*. Nashville, TN: Abingdon.

Howard, T. A., & Howard, S. (1992). *Kids ending hunger*. Kansas City, MO: Andrews and McMeel.

Hubbard, J. (1991). *Shooting back: A photographic view of life by homeless children*. San Francisco: Chronicle.

Kaufman, C., & Kaufman, G. (1987). *Hotel boy*. New York: Macmillan.

Rosen, M. J. (Ed.). (1992). *Home*. New York: HarperCollins.

Tolan, S. (1992). *Sophie and the Sidewalk Man*. New York: Macmillan.

Wezeman, V., Aalsburg Wiessner, P., & Aalsburg Wiessner, C. (1991). *Benjamin Brody's backyard bag*. Illinois: Brethren Press/Faithquest.

Wine, J. (1989). *Silly Tillie*. Intercourse, PA: Good Books.

Share Our Strength (SOS) is a nonprofit organization whose goal is to make nutritious food available to needy people, particularly the homeless. For information, write to Share Our Strength, 1511 K St. NW, Suite 600, Washington, DC 20005.

CHAPTER SEVEN

MAKING MEANING IN READING, WRITING, ART, MUSIC, AND DRAMA

Before reading, consider...
- *All the ways you make and appreciate meaning in your life (e.g., reading, writing, art, music, and dance).*
- *How frequently you encourage students to explore ideas in other ways besides language.*

Story 1: Beginning the Journey

When Karen Capitani was beginning as a primary teacher many years ago, she spent a great deal of time thinking about, reading about, and talking about the things that young children do naturally—particularly all the wonderful and diverse ways they spontaneously express themselves. One summer she observed her kindergarten-age niece closely. The reading and writing and playing parts were immediately visible: her niece was very social, loved being with her friends, enjoyed books as a big part of her life, and had just discovered the power of writing (there were notes to Mom, Dad, and the dog scattered around the house). But there were other things: Karen's niece moved through her days singing, dancing, drawing, coloring, and playing an old harmonica she had found in the basement. Karen thought one of her niece's behaviors was especially charming. She would waltz up to her aunt, swinging her arms broadly, get very close to her and then share one secret thought or a quick story ("Aunt Karen, did you know . . . ?"). Then she would *dance* away. Although Karen knew the simple joy of movement that children displayed, these movements didn't seem arbitrary to Karen. Often, they seemed to be consciously *choreographed*, extending directly from the idea or thought or feeling her niece had been entertaining.

These behaviors, Karen observed, were often just little snippets sprinkled throughout the day, but what impressed Karen, now that she was watching, was that they were sprinkled throughout the *entire* day. Her niece was at once a dancer, an artist, an actress, a reader, a writer, and a musician. All of this dove-tailed with Karen's interest and belief about how children make sense of the world. While she felt her first-grade classroom already provided some opportunities for her students to express their thinking in different ways, they certainly weren't as available on an ongoing basis as they needed to be. She wanted her classroom to more closely match the multiple kinds of learning that her observations and conversations with children were revealing.

That summer she also attended a curriculum workshop. One choice of activities during the day was to read a children's book with a partner, talk about it, and then draw an interpretation to share. Karen chose *Faithful Elephants,* a startling story about a Tokyo zoo during World War II in which three beloved elephants are starved to death because the city feared that if the bombs hit the zoo, the animals would escape and run wild in the city. During her conversation with her partner, she focused on the heartbreak the zookeepers felt as they withheld food from the elephants. Karen felt a similar heartbreak as she read about the elephants pitifully begging for food by performing their banzai trick—something that had always been rewarded in the past. As Karen sketched, her original focus on the individual incident described in the story broadened and deepened to include the horrors of war for every living thing.

Through her reflection, she became aware of how her initial thinking changed as a result of the art experience itself. In the past, she had asked her students to respond in writing to the literature they heard or read. Art was reserved for drawing a favorite part. Now she had a simple strategy she could put into place, and she hoped it would help her students deepen their understandings and provide a new way to represent them.

In the fall, she encouraged her students to respond to literature by drawing their meanings. She followed the same procedure she had used during the workshop: choice of books, talking with a partner, drawing, and sharing. She always made a range of art materials available to choose from, and, even though she bemoaned her lack of artistic ability, she continually demonstrated her own responses to books by joining different partners to discuss the literature and then creating a sketch, collage, or other art form.

One day Karen read *The Name of the Tree* to her class. In this story, there was a drought, and a group of animals are on the verge of starvation. One at a time, the animals go to the wise lion to find out the name of the tree so it will lower its lush branches to give them food, but only a young, determined tortoise succeeds in remembering the name of the tree and bringing it back to the group. After reading, Karen asked, "What did the story mean to you? What was it really all about?"

At this point in the year, Karen's students were accustomed to these questions and they knew she was encouraging them to come up with their own personal interpretations—what was important to them or what the story made them think about. She kept an eye on Alex, because he rarely volunteered during these discussions after reading, even less often when she asked them to respond by writing in their journals. His journal was filled with beautiful, detailed sketches, but only a few attempts at words. Initially, she praised all of his art, but later, she thought that he should be writing more. Now, with the rethinking she had been doing about trying to value all forms of expression more, she began to wonder if Alex would come to writing more happily if she allowed him to consistently draw on this strength a while longer:

> The whole thing with Alex made me very nervous. I had always felt that my real job in first grade was to teach them to read—and begin to write. Even though I wanted them to express themselves more in other forms, putting art and writing on the same level seemed like a whole different ballgame to me, but after my observations and reflections, I knew there

Sketch to Stretch

Supplies:

- Multiple copies of a reading selection
- Pencil, paper, and crayons or colored markers

1. Students should be divided into small groups of four or five.

2. After reading the selection, students should think about what they read and then draw a sketch of "what the selection meant to you or what you made of the reading."

3. Students should be told there are many ways of representing the meaning of an experience and they are free to experiment with their interpretation. Students should not be rushed but given ample time to read and draw.

4. When the sketches are complete, each person in the group shows his or her sketch to the others in that group. The group participants study the sketch and say what they think the artist is attempting to say.

5. Once everyone has been given the opportunity to hypothesize an interpretation, the artist, of course, gets the last word.

6. Sharing continues in this fashion until all group members have shared their sketches. Each group can then identify one sketch in the group to be shared with the entire class. This sketch is put on an acetate sheet for the overhead projector.

Reference: Harste, J. C., & Short, K. G. (1988). *Creating classrooms for authors.* Portsmouth, NH: Heinemann. (pp. 353–354).

was something right about it. I began to feel that maybe Alex was the acid test for the changes I was trying.

During the discussion, David said he thought the book was about what it's like to be hungry and how sad it is (most likely responding to the sentence, "The animals sat on the ground and cried because the fruit smelled so good and they were so hungry"). Maria said it made her think of the lion in *The Lion, the Witch, and the Wardrobe* because her mom had just read it to her. Dana said it was about how you should keep trying. This time Alex ventured a tentative response: "I think it's about how the tortoise remembered the name of the tree." After a few more responses, Karen passed around drawing paper and asked her students to choose colored pencils or markers to sketch their pictures.

Amid the rustling of paper and searching for crayons and markers, there was one raised hand. "Ms. Capitani?" "Yes, Ryan?" "Could I draw my picture with Alex? He's a better drawer than I am." She hesitated. Her intent had been for them to express their own personal ideas about the story, and she didn't really want Alex to do all of the drawing; then Ryan wouldn't have the opportunity to construct his own meaning in art. However, she had told them many times before that it was helpful to think with someone else. "OK, but I'd like for you to talk about how you can both work on the drawing together. Let me know if you need some help." She watched them put their heads together.

Alex's interpretive drawing

"Anyone want to share?" Alex and Ryan had their hands waving before anyone else had completely heard the question. It seems that they had talked about the book and each decided to create their own pictures after all. Ryan's was a large tree weighted down with fruit and presents. He said that the tree had given the animals its best gifts, the way his mom and dad did for his birthday. Alex showed a picture of a large elephant standing next to the tree, surrounded by other animals. The elephant was saying, "I forgot." Alex explained that he often forgets, and so he wanted to draw the elephant doing the same thing: "But after I drew it, I thought about how I could say what I wanted to remember over and over again the way the tortoise did. I'm going to try it tomorrow with my mom."

Karen was struck not only by the personal connection Alex had made to the book, but also by the way the act of drawing his picture had helped him realize that he could try to solve his problem the same way the tortoise had—with determination.

The next morning, Alex wrote in his journal about the drawing. He didn't write much, but it was the beginning of a steady, increased willingness to express himself alternately in writing and art throughout the rest of the year.

After the Alex experience, Karen began to open up her classroom even more. She gradually restructured her teaching and the environment to include more ongoing informal opportunities for her children to think through ideas in music, art, and drama. She began to reorganize her classroom to include areas the children could go to throughout the day to experiment with art or music or, along with a few friends, practice a dramatization they could sign up to present to the class. She also wanted them to feel they had a range of responses to choose from when they read or heard books. On one occasion, she asked the art and music teachers to come into her classroom while she was reading a book aloud to the children and to join in their discussions. Then, she divided the class into thirds: the art teacher joined one group, the music teacher joined another, and she joined a third. Each group discussed the book and what they thought it meant, and then each worked to represent their thinking in art, music, or drama. Each teacher shared his or her own creative process—starting with an overall idea, thinking through alternatives, trying things out, revising, and constantly asking, "How close is my art/music/play to what I intended?" "Are my ideas changing as I go?"

After each group shared, they came together to reflect. David said, "I didn't know exactly what I thought the book meant until I started drawing. Then—there it was! Just coming out a little bit at a time!"

Sharon revealed, "Working with other people on the play made us think about how the mother might really look and how she might really sound. So we tried it out in lots of different ways until we decided that it would work."

Shandra decided, "The music was kind of hard. I didn't think we really made it sound like Michael Jackson (ha) but we thought we got the right *feeling*."

Karen was on her way. She knew she had a good, solid start toward developing the kind of curriculum that would help her students see and experience the world in all its wonder.

Story 2: Wildlife Symphony

Meaning in Multiple Forms All Day, Every Day

When first graders walk into Lynn White's classroom at the beginning of the school year, they are welcomed by a space that gives them an immediate idea of what to expect.

There is a platform for large group, small group, or individual performances, conferences, or ongoing project work; a block area that contains 500 unit blocks and a 7-by-3-foot mirror to help children see their constructions and themselves from multiple perspectives; a studio space with an easel and a table for working, a mirrored shelf to display projects, and a shelf with all the supplies an artist could dream of—collections of materials, tempera paints, acrylics, pastels, colored chalk, watercolors, markers, pencils, and so forth; a math shelf filled with games and manipulatives; a literature shelf for all the books that have been gathered for the latest theme or project (other literature is sorted by author, topic, genre, or level and fills the bins that are scattered around the room); a writing shelf where the children keep their journals and writing folders and books that are in the process of being illustrated; a bi-level wooden structure for individuals to have personal time and space; a multipurpose table used in the fall as a playdough table and later for a display or collection table; a shelf in the front for published books; three computers;

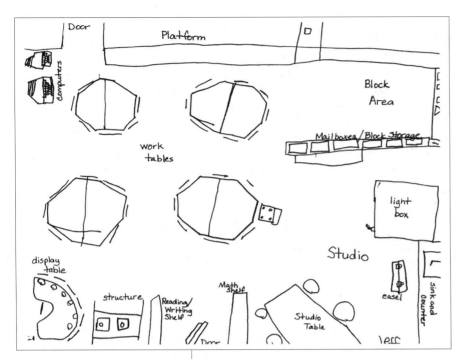

A child's drawing of Lynn's classroom arrangement.

another space on the floor for group meetings; and, outside the door, a sand table on a milk crate.

The room has the feel of a more grown-up, slightly formalized kindergarten or preschool classroom. Indeed, Lynn feels strongly that the first six weeks in first grade should be a transition time that has the familiar feel of the grade and developmental focus her children finished just a few short months before. The children have an immediate sense of security walking into this classroom, not only with the physical surroundings, but with materials as well. Lynn introduces the new parts of first grade slowly.

The first weeks of school are filled with major messages about the classroom and learning and living with many other people in a small space:

- Everyone and their ideas are important to making the classroom work.
- There must be respect for other people's ideas, work, and space.
- You will never be asked to do something that you cannot do.
- You have to take risks if you're going to learn.
- Everyone is expected to make thoughtful choices (different sets of criteria for choosing—from whom to sit with to what form to communicate in—are discussed and clarified throughout the year).
- *Everyone has inside of them the ability to be a reader, a writer, an artist, an actor and a musician, and everyone is expected to express themselves in multiple ways.*

At the beginning of each year, Lynn talks to the art, music, and P.E. teachers. Her goal is to have as many large blocks of time as possible. She doesn't mind if her students have two specials back to back as long as she, then, can have all of them for an extended time; she feels that anything less than an hour and a half makes it difficult for her six-year-olds to engage in the kind of thinking that is required when they are deeply involved in a project. Projects are usually characterized by children experiencing a topic through many of the following curricular forms—reading, writing, art, drama, music, math, and science. When a group of children wanted to study chameleons, they read nonfiction and fiction books, looked at photographs and drawings in science journals and magazines, observed their own classroom pet chameleon, sketched pictures, took observation notes, and shared their research by writing their own nonfiction book, which included sketches and watercolor paintings.

Every child in Lynn's classroom has an important piece of equipment—a clipboard. Often, you can walk into the classroom and see small figures clutching their clipboards importantly, intently observing some object and making notes and sketches, which will be used later to produce final writing or art.

This is the classroom and the context that was responsible for the creation of one spring's "Wildlife Symphony."

A group of five children came to Lynn and asked if they could go to the resource room; they needed to do research on deer, bears, and rabbits. They were worried that these animals were becoming endangered because "so many people want rabbit fur, deers' antlers, and bears' skin and bears' blubber so they can eat it."

While Lynn was used to her children banding together to pursue topics of common interest, an outsider might see this as an unlikely alliance. First there was Alison, who played the violin and was competent in all academic areas. Next was Beth, who, even though she was new to the school this year, was socially popular and a class leader. Then came Amanda, who was repeating first grade, had lost her mother during the year, and had been diagnosed with three different learning disabilities. Kuhn did not speak or understand any English at the beginning of the year, but by the springtime, he could understand most of what was said to him and was making strides in his expressive language. Finally, there was tiny Meagan, well-rounded in all social, emotional, and academic ways.

This was the first time this group had worked together, but each child knew of the others' interest in animals and had decided they should find out more about these particular ones. Alison explained later that, at first, they were just going to find out about the animals and talk to the class. However, as their reading, talking, and research progressed, they knew they had to draw the animals as well and show their movements, or their classmates wouldn't understand completely what they were talking about or why it was so important. Putting it all to music just seemed like it would fit, a natural idea in a classroom where students were accustomed to presenting their thinking in diverse forms.

The wildlife group gathered books and began to read. As they talked about what they wanted to show their classmates about these animals, they began to develop a deeper understanding about why these animals (or any animals) needed to be protected. Meagan reported that "first we just had this idea about these animals, but then when we started finding things out about them and choosing what we wanted to show in our drawings and what we wanted to act out, we knew that it was *really* important to keep them alive. I mean, they have *different* ways of moving and they all belong to a *family*."

As the group worked, Lynn occasionally stopped by to consult with them about their progress and to help them see the network of hard and careful choices they were making: "How's it going?" "What are you doing?" "What are you thinking now?" Then she would watch them plow back into their work.

Lynn could see that no source of thinking was acting alone; reading led to drawing and acting, but if they were not quite right, the group was compelled to rethink, reread, and revise. "They were finding out that although discovery can be magic, it can also be demanding work. I watched them start with a compelling but fairly general idea. As they investigated and tried things out, their idea took on a more clear and definite shape."

The wildlife group spent two weeks researching and preparing to share their ideas. Every day for 45 minutes during the afternoon choice time, they read books, selected specific segments they wanted to share, drew pictures of the animals from different perspectives, and practiced dramatizing different portions of the written material (animal movements, animal playfulness, mother-baby interactions). During the practice session, Alison suddenly said, "This should be a symphony! I can bring my violin and it will help us show how the rabbits and deer move fast and how the bear cubs play. I can compose music to go with the words and movement." Not everyone was sure what a symphony was, but after Alison explained how the different sections work together and sketched a picture of the strings, brass, and woodwinds, they seemed to understand. It was agreed. For the next few days Lynn could hear the stops and starts, high notes, low notes, and occasional screeches as Alison created and revised music to

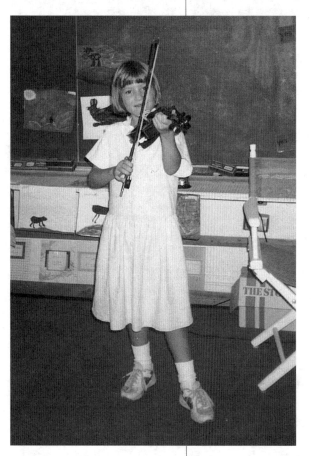

accompany the art, drama, and readings.

When they were ready for the performance, the group informed Lynn, and she asked them what they needed to make it a success. Their only requests were for space to display their pictures and for enough room to do the actual performance. Lynn asked for permission to videotape.

At the designated time, the first-grade audience assumed their sitting positions on the floor. Alison walked onto the stage carrying her violin and a serious expression. Beth and Amanda followed, while Kuhn and Meagan were hidden under a nearby table waiting for their first cue to appear on all fours.

First came the deer, then the bears, and finally the wild rabbits. Each time, Beth read while Alison played and Kuhn and Meagan acted out their different roles. The music changed noticeably each time a new animal was introduced: the deer were expressed by a slow, fluid sound; the bears (evidently cubs) were playful and were accompanied by a matching, quick pace; and the wild rabbits had their own wild music—a little screechy with less of an identifiable rhythm than the other animals.

When the final notes faded, the group took multiple bows and the audience applause went on and on. Lynn asked everyone to respond. Many of the comments were like Tamar's: "I didn't think much about these animals before, but they all have special ways of moving and they all love their mothers. We have to make sure they don't die."

The class gave the wildlife group much more than applause; they asked Lynn right away if they could create their own animal symphonies. Not long after the widely talked about Wildlife Symphony, there was, complete with a written text, dramatization, and first-grade-designed costumes, a Dinosaur Symphony complete with a Stegosaurus Symphony, a T-Rex Symphony, a Brontosaurus Symphony, and an Ankylosaurus Symphony.

Reflective Commentary

We learn from the wildlife group that they started out with a common interest, decided to get together to study the animals they were concerned about, and initially intended to share their learning by talking about what they had found. Evidently, at some point in their research, they decided that saying what they knew only through language wasn't enough—their talk would be better if they acted it out, they should show what the animals look like by drawing them from different perspectives, and finally, there should be music to bring the whole thing to life. Not just any old music— it had to be a *symphony!* Any animal would be honored.

These first graders attend a classroom where communicating meaning in multiple forms is simply what goes on every day. They are learning to think differently than do children who have limited opportunities to express themselves in art and music and drama, differently than children who go to art and music classes once or twice a week and dramatize a play here and there. Lynn White's children are immersed in a curriculum that nurtures the expression of meaning in all the ways that are dominant in our culture: dance, music, visual arts, and of course, the expected forms of reading, writing, and math.

Eisner (1990) underscores the idea of a broad-based definition of literacy. If literacy means the ability to construct and secure meaning, the term cannot only refer to reading and writing: "Not everything that we want to say can be said in language. Not everything that we want to convey can be reported in number" (p. 15). Eisner warns that if we ignore these multiple forms of literacy, we are guaranteed to produce students who are at best semi-literate. Other educators (Berghoff, 1993; Gardner, 1983; Leland & Harste, 1994; Short, 1990) join Eisner in underscoring the dangers of an overemphasis on language to the exclusion of other ways of thinking and knowing.

In talking about her classroom and teaching, Lynn White says, "My classroom reflects the way children think and learn. I believe that children are innately capable and curious and have multiple ways of thinking, knowing, and communicating what they know and understand. It's my job to offer them multiple opportunities to do these things. When I encourage them to think, explore, and reflect, the more they can represent and communicate, the stronger and richer are their understandings."

When asked about her role in the classroom, she says, "Well, first, my role is to be clear on my philosophy. My classroom practice comes from that philosophy but my practice also influences my philosophy. They are intertwined all the time and you can't separate them. It is my thinking about this relationship and its implications that keeps me growing professionally."

Lynn also believes that observing children and responding to them while they are learning is a big part of being an effective teacher. "If I watch closely while my children are studying, researching, and experimenting, I can gain a window into their thinking. If I can do that, I can respond to what they are doing and ask questions that can help move them forward. I feel strongly about empowering them to be learners—teach them *how* to be learners, not just first-grade academic skills. I also want them to understand that their ideas are important and they can make their ideas come true, but also that their ideas can change when they read or write or draw or act or think."

Lately, Lynn has been focusing on the power of documentation and close observation. "Before, I thought I was a good listener but now I feel I hear so much more. I think that's because I am thinking more in terms of children's theories about the world and how I can connect their theories, ideas, and interests into first-grade skills, concepts, and curriculum. I'm learning more and more about different kinds of documentation. I used to take just video and photographs fairly often, but almost at random—when I thought something interesting was going to happen in the classroom, I would grab one camera or another. Now, I have added audio, and I am much more purposeful. When there is an experience I want to capture, I ask myself: 'What do I want to document and what form do I want to use?' This is exactly what happens with the children and the ways I encourage them to choose materials to represent different meanings—'What do you want to show?' and 'What is the best way?' I think teachers who are just beginning with these ideas should spend time watching and listening to children and then collaborating with colleagues about what they are seeing and hearing to figure out where they should go next."

Teachers often announce that they cannot teach art because they can't draw a straight line. But Karen's entry into a multiple-ways-of-knowing curriculum began with an understanding of the need for opportunity, not with an advanced fine arts degree. Diane Stephens (1994) says,

> The children in our classrooms deserve to understand about art and about being artful, and we, their teachers, need to teach them, even if what that means is that, as teachers, we learn along with them.

Another educator notes,

> We do not have to be professional artists or actors or musicians to help our children expand their literate abilities in these directions. But, because we are professional educators who understand the value of meaningful experience, we have to provide ongoing opportunities for children to express themselves in these multiple forms. Lest someone should accuse us of "soft" standards, remind them that the complexity of thought and the critical stance required to construct meaning in reading and writing are like those we engage when we create or respond to art. (Alejandro, 1994)

As Eisner points out, though, meaning in alternate sign systems is nonredundant—the meaning available to us in art is different than that of music and dance. The reasons for these systems' existence is to give us access to the world in diverse forms.

Leland and Harste (1994) offer a new definition of literacy: "A truly literate person is one who can mediate his or her world through multiple sign systems—not just language" (p. 344). These authors suggest that, historically, our language arts programs have focused far more on language than on arts and that, in the future, we need a new standard, one that expands rather than narrows communication potential.

What Key Standards Emerge and Interact in This Context?

Students read a range of print and nonprint texts. Students in Karen's class read and listened to a range of picture books and responded to them in multiple ways: through writing, art, music, and drama. They created and shared alternate interpretations of the books they read.

Students created and interpreted meanings through art, dance, and music. The wildlife group read, discussed, and selected specific information related to the animals they were researching. They presented their inquiry by integrating language, art, music, and drama.

Students read a range of literature in many genres. Students in Karen's classroom listened to and read literature in many different forms: poetry, picture books, nursery rhymes, and wordless picture books. Students responded to literature by voicing opinions, connecting to personal experience and related literature, journal writing, and drawing. Students regularly identified and talked about what was significant for them in a particular piece. Students in Karen's and Lynn's classrooms often represented their individual interpretations through art. Both classrooms gave opportunities for students to choose different media so they could explore their visual representations using watercolor, markers, crayon, and chalk.

Students apply a range of strategies. All students learned to make personal connections and individual interpretations of text. They used written, artistic, musical, and oral presentations to explore and express their meanings. Their creations and interpretations were often complex orchestrations of many strategies whose purpose was to see whole-to-part relationships and understand how communication in different forms work together to complement and create a whole.

The wildlife group selected information from nonfiction material and combined it with art, music, and drama to help them convey a specific message about endangered animals.

Students use knowledge of language structure, language conventions, media techniques, and genre. While creating the Wildlife Symphony, students made cross-disciplinary connections as they used their knowledge of how art elements are organized, how the conventions of music (tempo, volume) communicate different feelings and movement, and how the structure of a symphony can be used, along with written text, to send a specific message. Students' group process included drafting, revising and editing in writing, art, music, and drama.

Alex and his classmates experimented with various art techniques and organizations to express their interpretations of literature.

Students research issues and interests. Students in the wildlife group initiated research about deer, bears, and rabbits. As they read and discussed information about the animals, the groups' concern for their "endangered" status led them to revise their general questions to more specific ones about movement and family. Their research process included not only reading, writing, and talking, but also drawing, composing music, and acting. They orchestrated the message they wanted to communicate to their peers by using drama, art, and music in a balanced, supportive way, each expression representing their main ideas in a different way.

Students participate in a variety of literacy communities. Students in both classrooms participated in literacy experiences by collaborating in pairs, working in small groups, and participating in entire class activities. In Karen's classroom, students teamed up with the music or art teacher to learn the language of those expressions. In Lynn's classroom, the wildlife group researched and composed together over a period of weeks with each member contributing their own expertise (e.g., art, music) while also collaborating with other members of the group to move forward toward a common vision.

Students use spoken, written, and visual language to accomplish their own purposes. Students talk about the songs they are composing at home or the words they are writing to fit existing music. In class, they make tentative plans to go to one another's homes to create plays and compose music together. Because field trips are a strong part of the curriculum, parents report taking their children on weekends to revisit places like museums and art galleries. As they do in school, children who have home computers often use them independently to research topics of interest.

References and Other Resources

Alejandro, A. (1994). Like happy dreams—Integrating visual arts, writing, and reading. *Language Arts, 71*(1), 12–21.

Berghoff, B. (1993). Moving toward aesthetic literacy in the first grade. In D. J. Leu & C. K. Kinzer (Eds.), *Examining central issues in literacy research, theory, and practice* (pp. 217–233). Chicago, IL: National Reading Conference.

Bredekamp, S. (1993). Reflections on Reggio Emilia. *Young Children, 49*(1), 13–18.

Clyde, J. A. (1994). Lessons from Douglas: Expanding our visions of what it means to "know." *Language Arts, 71*(1), 22–33.

Edwards, C., Gandini, L., & Forman, G. (Eds.). (1993). *The hundred languages of children.* Norwood, NJ: Ablex.

Egawa, K., & Hoonan, B. (1994). Living a multiple ways of knowing curriculum: The challenges and rewards of putting literacy theory into practice. Presented at the National Council of Teachers of English Annual Conference, Orlando, FL.

Eisner, E. (1990). Implications of artistic intelligences for education. In W. J. Moody (Ed.), *Artistic intelligences: Implications for education* (pp. 31–42). New York: Teachers College Press.

Gardner, H. (1983). *Frames of mind: The theory of multiple intelligences.* New York: Basic Books.

Leland, C. H., & Harste, J. C. (1994). Multiple ways of knowing: Curriculum in a new key. *Language Arts, 71*(5), 337–345.

Short, K. (1990). Learning: Making connections across sign systems. Miami Beach, FL: National Reading Conference.

Stephens, D. (1994). Learning that art means. *Language Arts, 71*(1), 34–37.

CHAPTER EIGHT

NARRATIVE WRITING: TOWARD A "REAL KID" REPORT CARD

Before reading, consider . . .
- *What kind of information you find most valuable when someone is responding to your thinking and/or professional efforts.*
- *The relationship between your language arts curriculum and the reporting system currently in place.*
- *What contribution students make to formal reports about their learning.*

The evaluation component of the story shared here began in 1992 as a year-long inquiry in collaborative partnership with Kathy Egawa, Debbie Kavanaugh, Judy Best, and Debbie Edwards. Debbie, Judy, and Debbie were teaching in a small school involved in restructuring; Kathy worked with them for sixteen months while conducting her graduate research, "When Teachers Inquire." Now, several years later, Kathy has returned to teaching in the Seattle area, but their conversations and inquiry continue.

For many years over her eighteen-year-long career in special education and primary classrooms, Kathy's teaching had moved toward a more child-centered curriculum. She began by keeping daily dialogue journals with each student as a way of getting to know them and their interests. The basal scripts and drill lessons, which felt contrived and artificial, were replaced with texts that better engaged the interests and demographics of her inner-city classroom (e.g., *The Superkids*). Skills work played a supporting role rather than a primary one in her classroom.

Kathy pushed herself to create flexible groupings for instruction to help build the confidence of her less capable readers. Several years before taking a sabbatical for graduate study, she made a major shift similar to Eileen's, and replaced the reading textbooks with sets of children's literature. The tension that had pushed her through each of these changes now settled on evaluation. As she participated with her first graders in discussions about books, it became even *more* difficult to assign a level to her students' reading abilities. Errol, for example, who was frequently absent and just beginning to read, often led his group's discussions. Formerly a child who had participated little in his kindergarten class, he was now judged by a third of his peers as "having the best ideas" during their book conversations. How could Kathy fit this growing ability into a "reading level"? Then there was Stephanie, a child whose scores dipped on the "reading comprehension" section of the California Test of Basic Skills but who regularly scripted dramas to share her groups' discussions of their books. Further complicating these observations, Kathy noted that many of the students were reading, in the context of their literature choices, the Dolch words that they couldn't identify on the lists used to screen their abilities. Kathy felt frustrated and unable to tackle the district's reporting system alone. Seeing no obvious alternative, she continued to assign the *Outstanding, Satisfactory,* and *Needs Improvement* grades on the student report cards. She strived to consider "effort" as much as "ability" and felt compromised by the whole endeavor.

During her graduate study, however, Kathy had the opportunity to engage her beliefs about the limitations of traditional graded report cards. Working with teachers in a school committed to exploring narrative reports as part of a restructuring process, the journey she began with these colleagues also started with feelings of tension—first, the tension felt by the small school community electing to create more relevant, meaningful reporting instruments, more closely aligned to their curricular changes; and second, the tension of knowing that it wasn't possible to simply borrow reporting instruments from others or to create a perfect instrument themselves. The fact that the teachers were *choosing* to create change rather than being pressured into it made all the difference, though, and moved the school community forward.

The four colleagues confidently acknowledged that grades and standardized tests couldn't possibly provide accurate information about the complexity of the learning their students were engaged in. They talked about incidents from their own school experiences in which they had been evaluated (and misevaluated) by others. They talked about how it felt to have no voice in how their work was judged. They recognized that scores and comments did not feel "authentic" and did not capture the thinking or reading/writing strategies being used in different ways for different purposes. But they didn't know what to put in their place.

Because this group of teachers recognized that their understanding and perspectives would change as they worked, they knew (as did the entire school staff of nine teachers) to keep their work open to ongoing revision. They also knew they weren't likely to "get it right," regardless of the thoughtfulness of their work. Lastly, they acknowledged that for assessment to become more meaningful, it needed to be multidimensional, like the learning going on in their classrooms.

The school's experience with narratives began six months before Kathy joined them. In November 1991, with minimal preparation, the teachers faced blank computer screens and literally began to write. The first reports averaged three to four legal-length pages per student. The comments, organized by subjects, alternated between the curriculum activities of that reporting period, the teacher's expectations, and the student's performance. Here is an example from one area of one report:

Language Arts

I am very pleased with the increased interest and improvement that Chris has made in reading. A couple weeks ago he had two books ready to read with me after recess. I was so impressed. He has really gotten into the Mercer Mayer books lately (e.g., *Just a Mess*). He and I have been reading *Charlie and the Chocolate Factory* together. You might check it out from the library to finish with him. I have attached a paper that shows the "stages" a child progresses through when learning to read. Chris has shown incredible improvement. I feel that he demonstrated characteristics of the "magical stage" and "self-concepting stage" when school started and is now demonstrating characteristics of the "bridging stage." He can write and read back his own work, pick out some individual words and most letters now, read predictable books, is becoming more excited about reading and wants to read to others often, and most important of all, realizes that words have meaning.

Although everyone acknowledged that the students were better known as learners than ever before, the first narrative reports were unwieldy for both parents and teachers. First, teachers did all of the writing and conferencing outside the school day, as no school time was allocated for either activity, and narrative reports were much more time-consuming than the former report cards. Further, the teachers guessed that many parents in the community were not confident readers, and the new reporting form required a lot of reading. In subsequent discussions about students, it appeared some parents hadn't read their children's reports at all. In addition, the information wasn't organized so that indications of the students' ability and success were clear. Despite the lengthy and informative reports, several parents continued to ask, "How is she doing?", others expressed more confidence in letter grades, and still others expressed frustration with the "positive" tone to the report that didn't give them a focus to work on: "Yeah, but what is he *bad* at?" Perhaps, for the first time, parents who had not previously responded to the invitation to be involved in the report card overhaul came face-to-face with the evidence of substantial change.

Somewhat more common, however, was lack of response to the report cards. This was not the response expected after the time and energy the teachers spent writing! They forged ahead and continued the lengthy descriptions. During one of their group meetings, Debbie Kavanaugh confided: "When it's time to do the progress reports, I get stumped and I ask myself, 'What do I know about this kid?' You know what I mean? I just sit there sometimes and kind of freeze." Again, this tension cut across many issues, both practical and philosophical. "I'd feel more comfortable [with evaluating students] if I really knew what I was looking for and I could express that to parents."

During the second year of the restructuring efforts, the school "Leadership Team" responded to the teachers' wishes to schedule goal-setting conferences in the fall and spring, with the narrative reports coming out in January and June. They also responded to some parents' wishes that letter grades be provided on request (an option that had always been available). The revised assessment calendar provided the teachers with additional time to think more carefully about their own beliefs and expectations and time to consider feedback from parents. At Carolyn Burke's suggestion, they now tried listing indicators for the various curricular areas of the curriculum. Comments that the teacher had included under the lengthy "Language Arts" section, for example, were now divided into curriculum engagements: Classroom Newspaper, Newsboard, Dialogue Journal, Personal Journal, Literature Study, Buddy Reading, and Reading Strategies.

Debbie (Kavanaugh) and Kathy first began the long and thoughtful work of creating the list of indicators under each of these areas. They sat together in the university computer lab, named one curriculum activity, and then separately listed what they thought were significant things to look for. After five or ten minutes, they shared their lists and meshed them into one. After many hours,

Reflective Questions on Reporting

- What am I supposed to watch or collect?
- How can I take notes effectively?
- How should we organize the progress reports?
- What if different teachers' reports don't look the same?
- How do I evaluate without giving a negative sense of the process?
- Who is evaluation really for?

they came up with an initial "frame" which Debbie used for her winter reporting. The first draft of the literature study section that was used with students in two of the multiage primary classrooms included the following points of consideration:

Literature Study

The student . . .

- signs up for book of choice
- participates in discussion by: making personal connections, making connections with other stories, asking questions about the text and illustrations, discusses with other group members
- listens to the story on tape and follows along
- contributes to the plans and extension activities
- negotiates with friends how to share the book
- follows along with the reading of the book (based on his or her ability)
- reads book for homework
- presents his or her ideas to the class

Specific comments about each child were then included below these statements. A written introduction to the new form was included at the top of the report and parents were asked to give feedback. The responses from the parents who responded were heartening:

> Now I understand what's expected of the children!

> We feel this was a thorough progress report. We also need to set up a conference with you. The indicators were excellent and we do appreciate so much all that you are doing for Ellie this year. Thank you for your comments about her.

> The indicators were a great help. I've often wondered how you used each item to assess. It shows how much individual time is given! Thanks for trying to get Erik working with other kids. I hate to sound so particular but he doesn't always make the best choices. Erik doesn't have a comment so I am enclosing a couple of stories he has written at home. They are first copies but I thought you would like to see them. I would like them back. Thanks for all your hard work and time given. I'm very pleased.

> Heatherann is doing much better at home, she is getting along with the family better but I have problems getting her to lower her voice and not yell at people. But she is doing better at it. I thank you Mrs. Edwards for being there.

> I am glad to see Donny is making some progress. I'm hoping he will even do much better. We are trying to help him more at home. I do believe the way you laid out the report helped us.

Initially, these forms included space for comment from the teacher, the parents, and the student at the end of the report, yet one student's father squeezed comments along the margins of each description area. When Debbie commented that she would like to see Larry contribute more detailed news on the daily newsboard, his father responded, "I think before nobody said much about school to him, therefore he didn't think school was no big deal." When she commented

**Language Arts:
Curriculum Engagements**

- Classroom newspaper
- Newsboard
- Dialogue journal
- Personal journal
- Literature study
- Buddy reading
- Reading strategies

that the handwriting in Larry's journal could be neater, he laughingly noted, "Larry gets in a hurry, but he is getting lots better. I think he has a lot more confidence and will get better if we show we care. P.S. My handwriting is pretty sloppy too, ha ha!" Throughout the report he'd responded to his son and himself as learners and helped the teachers better understand the larger learning context of Larry's life. They knew that Larry enjoyed writing stories about animals, but not that "Larry loves animals, he likes to go hunting with me [his father]."

The addition of these comments brought new life and importance to the physical layout of the report. When Debbie Edwards called to tell Kathy that the report almost "begged" a response, they revised the format to include space for comment throughout. In addition, they were pleased that parents had begun to envision other roles for themselves. Erik's mother sent in a story in lieu of personal comments from him; she and Heatherann's mother shared their own vulnerability with successful parenting.

The following school year, Kathy returned to the classroom and was teaching in a primary multiage program. She briefly revised the form the group had created the year before. Kathy was now personally experiencing the reporting challenges of her Indiana collaborators. Although her class size was larger and she had more reports to write, her school system did provide one day each reporting period to write reports, four half days in the fall to conference with parents, and four "planning days" that could be used each year at the teacher's discretion (these days were "earned" by taking lunch duty, thus allowing for the reallocation of school funds to substitute pay). Nonetheless, looking through each student's work, referring to the anecdotal notes she'd taken during the reporting period, and writing significant comments for 25 students was an overwhelming task. It was difficult to write thoughtful comments in a short period of time for so many students; she also found that writing for each curriculum activity was often redundant—for instance, she could focus on writing with several specific examples, rather than discussing writing in response journals or notebooks. In the meantime, during each reporting period, curriculum in the classroom took a back seat for several weeks. She wasn't confident that the time spent writing the narratives was spent well or that her comments were the most helpful to students and parents.

Kathy ended that school year with a new goal: a commitment to add a "learning profile" to the reporting process. While she valued the narrative reporting process, especially as it informed her own understanding of the students as learners, she felt it was important to provide a larger picture for parents and other educators—something other than test scores or a skills sequence—that illustrated where their children were working in relation to a broader "developmental" learning process. She was also interested in adding documentation that was less time-consuming, as she imagined few school communities would elect to work with narratives in the form she and her colleagues were currently working with. She began with the area of reading and with several "profile" documents created by other educators. As she had experienced with her colleagues, directly borrowing other documents didn't seem possible. After four years of study in the field of literacy, she could now recognize reading behaviors that other educators had not included in profiles of reading. For instance, by letting the students' interests and expertise take the lead, rather than the textbooks, she had seen children exhibit strengths she had not witnessed before. Craig, a first grader who was not yet reading independently, nonetheless responded to his classmates' interests with books and magazines from the class library, the school library, and his collection at home. He read the sophisticated illustrations in the

Eyewitness series, for instance, to inform his own interests as well as those of nearly every student in the classroom. Kathy added this behavior to the profile. After six months of working with the profile in draft form, she used this document in conjunction with the goal setting conferences and the narrative reports later in the school year. Her kindergarten teacher colleagues, in particular, reported that the parents of their students responded favorably to this larger picture of how reading ability develops.

In the spring of 1995, Kathy agreed to be part of a day-long workshop on assessment with several of the authors of this volume. She chose to look closely at a student named Scott. Kathy had talked with Linda Crafton some months before to try to understand Linda's definition of inquiry-based evaluation, and she soon understood that this was the push she needed to include more of the learner's perspective. While this had been part of her previous inquiry, she had not yet focused on adding the *learner's* comments to the formal written report.

She began with a series of questions that would help her add Scott's perspective of himself as a reader, writer, mathematician, and social studies/science learner. She then typed up Scott's written and verbal responses and added photographs of him in action, several of which she had taken at his direction. She

---

Scott as a Learner

READING & WRITING

My favorite books are:

Navy Fighters	50 Airplanes to Draw
Amazing Airplanes	Trouble With Trolls
The Way Things Work	Fighter Planes

I'm a good reader because I read books.
I kinda browse my magazines and car action books. I don't think I'm really good -- I'm OK. Usually I like to read with a friend; it helps me because I can't read every page. Anyway, it's 250 pages.

My favorite literature group was when we read Owl at Home.

We talked about what it was about and stuff.
About how owl wasn't very smart - like trying to be in 2 places at the same time - like crying about hardly anything - spoons behind the stove

INQUIRY PROJECTS

Sometimes we study topics together (different systems like the bicycle, identifying and classifying rocks, learning about magnets, calligraphy) and sometimes we choose our own topics. Here are three of my best projects: *I think those are my best studies:*

1. RC Cars
I did a good job on it. I was going to study frequencies but after I got my car I did both. I think my presentation was good.

2. Birds of Prey
I couldn't figure out how they could dive from so high at 200 mph - but if they put their wings all the way back they'd just whoosh them out. I've heard of some airplanes (Japanese ones) that have dive-break (nicknamed the Stuka) - they don't drop bombs, they throw them and they make a scream sound when they reach 100 mph - the flaps makes the sound. How can birds push their wings forward? I've heard birds have hollow bones, like hollowed out fingernails. Maybe it has fibers that make it sort of strong, maybe different kinds of calcium added together really tight.

3. Jets
Not my very best. I didn't talk loud enough. I didn't know near as much as I do now, well, like what the numbers [on the jets] stand for. When my dad was watching [my video] well he and Patty probably know a lot more than me. But I did know that Mach meant "speed of sound."

MY FUTURE PLANS

During the next couple months I want to be a better reader.
Read like more at school. Maybe study UFO's. I thought Max's presentation was interesting. I've seen lots of shows [about them] on Unsolved Mysteries.

Additional Comments

From a friend
Scott is nice to people. He knows times in math, and plus. He doesn't like me junking up the jets he sketches. He's a good reader - He can read *Trouble with Trolls* real good. Bryce

He likes to draw jets and he's a good freind. He's a good readers. He read one of the Fox books with me and Derrick and he was doing a good job with the pages that were harder for me and Derrick. He's really really good at soccer.

From my teacher
Last year you were just learning to read; now you can read pretty well. You're one of the best sketchers and your illustrations could go well in a book if you write one. Last year I didn't know you were so good at soccer or the piano! You sounded great playing with Mr. Gibbon. I want your 4th grade teacher to know how smart you are -- like on your Inquiry Projects.

From my parent(s) This has been a landmark year with Scott's leap forward in reading and other interests. Exciting and challenging! Mom

also collated a number of comments his classmates had made about him as a learner. Creating these documents, which she did between reporting periods, allowed her a closer look at Scott. This was somewhat surprising to her, as she had only recently looked across fourteen months of his work to prepare for a fall conference presentation. She knew of and valued Scott's abilities in art, music, building, and his longstanding aircraft inquiry, which had not been recognized or valued during his first two years in school. There were daily opportunities in the classroom for Scott to engage with the activities that he felt were challenging; yet, she hadn't solicited comments from Scott in the direct way that became her focus that spring.

By the end of the year, Kathy had again revised the formal written report to include the students' voices. She created a two-page list of questions that paralleled the format she and her colleagues used in their reports, and for a number of weeks, she worked with her first-, second-, and third-grade students to answer the questions, by themselves and in dictation to adults. When she sat down to write the June reports, she typed each student's responses into the reporting database prior to writing her own comments.

What a difference! Although it was the end of the year and she knew the first-grade students much better than she had earlier (the second and third graders had been with her for two years), their comments helped trigger her own stories of their engagement as learners. She knew she was getting closer to what she could not even have envisioned at the beginning of the journey. And her journey continues.

Reflective Commentary

Is there a school in this country that hasn't tackled the daunting challenge of revising their inhouse reporting system? More and more educators have been questioning the potential of a single letter grade to capture extended, complex learning. Educators often wonder about the validity of phrases like "comprehends at grade level" or "uses writing process." The reform efforts in which Kathy and her colleagues engaged focused on trying to tell parents more about children's learning, significant thinking behaviors, and identifiable developmental benchmarks. Similar efforts often proceed in a predictable manner. Committees charged with report card reform meet on a regular basis, examine other districts' work, bring in outside consultants, have many conversations about what is important to measure in reading/writing curricula, generate drafts for response from the faculty at large, painfully make the final decisions, print, distribute, and wait for parent response.

One thing that tends not to happen is raising the consciousness of the conflicting beliefs about learning that inevitably exist within any large group of educators. These underlying assumptions about teaching and learning have to be identified, so that discussion and reflection on them can lead to something other than superficial replacement of one set of descriptors for another. Burton (1991) points out that while we have experienced a virtual "renaissance" since the 1960s regarding how children learn language, we have changed very little about how that information is framed, developed and communicated to parents (p. 365).

Kathy and her colleagues began their journey with a tension about traditional assessment and ways of reporting that information. As Kathy points out, however, they began out of choice rather than mandate, and that makes all the difference in the longevity and quality of the journey. Choice here has far more to do with teachers bringing their questions and areas of discomfort to the surface; paying attention to those areas of curriculum that create an uncomfortable feeling. This is exactly the conscious state of inquiry that can help a teacher grow professionally (Watson, Burke, & Harste, 1989). What is your area of professional discomfort? What is, as Burke says, the "nightmare in your curriculum closet"? Answering that question can be the beginning of a period of tremendous insight and growth, but one must recognize, as Kathy did, that it will be a long, thoughtful effort, and that you must always keep your thinking open to ongoing revision. Professional growth is not about "getting it right," but it *is* about the excitement of finding new questions and thinking with others who have common goals.

In 1989, the National Association of Elementary School Principals published a list of tips for reducing report card stress. Responding to this list can make it far too easy to get pulled into the wrong argument ("Yes, it's a good idea to figure out ways to decrease the stress of report cards; after all, they can be real sources of anxiety for our kids"). The flashing red light in this instance—putting stress on children—prompts us to reexamine the question. The question is not how to reduce the stress that assessment reporting can cause, but rather, how to transform our reporting procedures so that they support learners and encourage their continued growth. Every school around the country could be asking what function our current evaluation procedures and reporting systems serve.

In its true, real-world form, there are a number of issues to keep in mind regarding evaluation:

- Evaluation is an integral part of a larger learning cycle (evaluation should be one more opportunity to learn);
- Evaluation is internal to the learner (evaluation should encourage learners to turn inward and think about what they have learned, how they have learned it, and what they want to do next);
- Evaluation works best when there are ongoing conversations about the meaning of key experiences.

(Crafton, 1994)

Evaluation, then, must be seen first and foremost as an opportunity to pull the learner into thinking about learning as it is occurring. Student reflection on the processes and products of learning should be the *primary information* that gets reported: to parents and to other teachers. Only then can we recognize whether children are growing in their abilities to self-evaluate; only then can we feel confident that we are growing in our abilities to elevate children's voices in every area of curriculum. Evaluation, like the national standards, cannot be something done *to* children. Just as Edelsky speaks of education *for* democracy, we must think about evaluation *for* learners rather than evaluation and reporting *about* learners.

One of the major issues that cannot be overlooked in assessment and evaluation is the simple fact that once a set of behaviors is designated as *the* most important, those behaviors become the primary behaviors that are valued, encouraged, and reported on. If we want our classrooms to be "experience-centered" instead of "objectives-centered," our reporting procedures must be open-ended enough to encourage that. In one draft of the narrative report Kathy and her colleagues produced, they structured their observations around key curricular components in the classroom: newspaper, journals, literature study, art, music, drama. Open-ended designations such as these encourage far more individual and diverse observations within various contexts than do specific skill checklists, which can produce a uniform profile of every student in the classroom.

Early in their assessment inquiry, Debbie Kavanaugh shared the frustration and immobility she sometimes felt when composing progress reports. At a recent inservice, many teachers shared the same miserable feeling, but added that it wasn't a lack of observational skills or documentation that accounted for it—they felt they had trouble differentiating. All their narratives about individual children sounded the same, from one reporting period to the next, and often there was great similarity from child to child. Interestingly, this was an impressive, knowledgeable group of teachers who were skilled "kidwatchers." So, what was the problem?

Discussions helped the group uncover the idea of "voiceless narratives." There seemed to be at least three major issues: a lack of verbatim statements and reflections from the learner, the absence of conversations with the learner prior to the narrative writing, and the absence of perspective from the learner in the narrative itself. As teachers, we can take voluminous anecdotal notes and make extended observations of children's learning in progress, but we alone cannot be the ones to determine the significance of a learning experience, and we cannot leave the learners out of the conversation and hope to stumble onto what is genuinely important to them. We must have evaluation conversations with all of our students. As Kathy points out, their comments helped trigger her own stories of their engagements as learners. Of course, portfolios have taught us a lot about the student role in reflection, documentation, and reporting. Indeed, Kathy notes that as student portfolios have evolved, the narrative report has actually taken on less significance.

Kathy shows us one wonderful interpretation of the idea of student voice in evaluation. Further along in her journey, she elevates reflection, evaluation, and reporting to a shared position. She begins to give her students *first* voice in the revised narrative, and, as she says, "What a difference!" Now the message to student and parents is transformed: The primary audience for evaluation and reporting is the learner. It is the student who can be encouraged to engage in an inner dialogue, one that Kathy begins to map out with the reflective questions she now asks of them.

With the addition of students to the narrative evaluations, Kathy has transformed a reporting procedure that initially belonged only to the teacher to one that is now filled with the life, the voice, and the uniqueness of the individual child. Her understanding, along with her visions and hopes of comprehensive assessment and increased student self-evaluation, continues to grow.

What Key Standards Emerge and Interact in This Context?

Students read a range of print and nonprint texts. Students in Kathy's classroom read newspapers, newsboard, dialogue journals and personal journals. Students use private and dialogue journals to draw as well as write. They engage in sustained silent reading and participate in literature discussions using fiction and nonfiction materials. Students explore and share self-selected topics through reading, talking, retelling stories, and writing their own texts.

Students read a wide range of literature in many genres. Kathy makes literature and inquiry cornerstones of her curriculum. Students read fiction, nonfiction, award-winning picture books, multicultural literature, classroom published books, and poetry. Kathy reads aloud to them daily, openly discussing strategies that she uses during reading and giving them opportunities to observe and share their own strategies.

Students apply a range of strategies. Students use a number of key strategies as they read: predicting using meaning, grammar and sound/symbol cues, confirming, rereading, skipping unknown words, substituting synonyms, or using picture cues. During writing, students select personal topics, draft, and publish their own stories. Scott uses art as a primary means of expressing his ideas. Learners are asked to identify social strategies (i.e., how they help each other) for supporting peers and strategies that are most useful to them when they were "stuck" in composing or comprehending.

Students adapt the conventions to communicate effectively. A range of language contexts gives Kathy's students the opportunity to use different spoken, written, and visual language conventions for different audiences. Students write in journals, alone, with one another, and for dialogue with the teacher. They use talk for book discussions, planning and implementing inquiry, and reflecting on themselves as readers, writers, researchers, presenters, and friends. Scott demonstrates the awareness of audience that is cultivated in Kathy's classroom when he reflects on his video presentation, how loudly he spoke and his knowledge level compared to those who were watching.

Students apply knowledge of language structure, language conventions, media techniques, and genre. Students write stories, letters, notes, video scripts, and directions. During these experiences, they experiment with spelling, punctuation, grammar, and larger text structure. They read a range of literature and nonfiction and discuss the differences in organization of these and other print materials. They respond to and critique commercially published materials and their own classroom-produced texts. Students explore various art forms and materials as they think through the ideas they want to represent as artists, architects, musicians, or actors.

Students research issues and interests. Kathy's students choose topics of personal interest to research. This is an area of engagement represented as a major curricular component on her most recent narrative report card.

Students use collaborative as well as individual inquiry to pursue topics. Students pose questions, gather resources (print and nonprint), select significant information, discuss findings and inquiry strategies, and, determine effective ways to communicate what they have learned. Students evaluate both the process and product of their research: How did things go during the research? What resources were helpful, not helpful? Was the sharing/presentation effective? How do you know?

Students participate in a variety of literacy communities. Students read with one another (buddy reading) and collaborate on different writing experiences (e.g., journals, stories, sketches with writing). Students work in pairs, small groups, and large groups to research topics of interest. Students take books home to read or share the reading with their parents or siblings. Students use e-mail to communicate with parents and other students. Literature discussions are an ongoing experience in Kathy's classroom—students join or create groups based on interest in an author, genre, or particular book.

Students use technological and information resources. Students produce videos to communicate their research. They use e-mail to talk to parents and other students. They access multimedia databases to support their individual and collaborative inquiries.

Students use spoken, written, and visual language to accomplish their own purposes. Parents in Kathy's classrooms report self-initiated reading and writing and inquiry. Scott made detailed sketches at home.

References and Other Resources

Burton, F. R. (1991). Reflections on designing a K–12 whole language curriculum: Implications for administrators and policy makers. In Y. Goodman & K. Goodman (Eds.), *Organizing for whole language*. Portsmouth, NH: Heinemann.

Campbell-Hill, B., & Ruptic, C. (1994). *Practical aspects of authentic assessment: Putting the pieces together*. Norwood, MA: Christopher-Gordon.

Cochrane, O., Cochrane, D., Scalena, S., & Buchanan, E. (1984).*Reading, writing and caring*. Winnipeg: Whole Language Consultants.

Copenhaver, J. (1993). Instances of inquiry. *Primary Voices, premier issue*, 6–14.

Crafton, L. K. (1994). *Challenges of holistic teaching: Answering the tough questions*. Norwood, MA: Christopher-Gordon.

Egawa, K., & Hoonan, B. (1994, November). *Living a multiple ways of knowing curriculum: The challenges and rewards of putting literacy theory into practice*. A presentation with J. Harste and B. Berghoff at the annual convention of NCTE, Orlando, FL.

Eisner, E. (1982). *Cognition and curriculum: A basis for deciding what to teach*. New York: Longman.

Harste, J. (1993). Literacy as curricular conversations about knowledge, inquiry, and morality. In M. Ruddell & R. Ruddell (Eds.), *Theoretical models and processes of reading* (4th ed.). Newark, DE: International Reading Association.

Johnston, P. H. (1992). *Constructive evaluation of literate activity*. Portsmouth, NH: Heinemann.

Siegel, M., & Carey, R. (1989). *Critical thinking: A semiotic perspective*. Urbana, IL: NCTE/ERIC.

Watson, D., Burke, C., & Harste, J. (1989). *Whole language: Inquiring voices*. Ontario: Scholastic.

AUTHOR

Linda K. Crafton began her professional career as a primary teacher and now consults in schools across the United States and Canada. She also teaches courses in reading and writing processes in the graduate program at Northwestern University. For ten years, Linda was a professor in the Department of Reading at Northeastern Illinois University.

Linda has published extensively. Her first book, *Whole Language: Getting Started . . . Moving Forward* (Richard C. Owen, 1991) has been described as "practical and inspiring . . . not to be missed!" Her second book, *Challenges of Holistic Teaching: Answering the Tough Questions* (Christopher-Gordon, 1994) tackles a wide range of authentic teacher concerns, including ability grouping, administrators, literature-based reading, evaluation, phonics, and teacher stress. Linda has also produced a set of audiotapes for parents describing beginning reading development. *A Lifetime of Success: Parents, Kids and Reading* (co-authored with Penny Silvers) helps parents understand reading as a naturally developing process and how their ongoing interactions with their children are key to proficiency and a lifelong love of reading. In 1994 Linda served as editor and contributing author for NCTE's *Primary Voices K–6* special issue on inquiry-based evaluation.

Linda lives in the Chicago area with her husband, Paul Katz, and their daughter, Samantha.

Other Books from NCTE Related to English Language Arts Content Standards

Standards for the English Language Arts

From the National Council of Teachers of English and the International Reading Association

What should English language arts students know and be able to do? This book—the culmination of more than three years of intense research and discussion among members of the English language arts teaching community, parents, and policymakers—answers this question by presenting standards that encompass the use of print, oral, and visual language and addresses six interrelated English language arts: reading, writing, speaking, listening, viewing, and visually representing. *Standards for the English Language Arts* starts by examining the rationale for standard setting—why NCTE and IRA believe defining standards is important and what we hope to accomplish by doing so. The book then explores the assumptions that underlie the standards, defines and elaborates each standard individually, and provides real-life classroom vignettes in which readers can glimpse standards in practice. Designed to complement state and local standards efforts, this document will help educators prepare *all* K–12 students for the literacy demands of the twenty-first century.   1996. Grades K–12. ISBN 0-8141-4676-7.
Stock No. 46767-4025
$18.00 nonmembers, $13.00 NCTE members

Standards Consensus Series

Books in this series serve as useful guides for K–12 teachers who are striving to align lively, classroom-tested practices with standards. A survey of local, state, and national documents revealed a broad consensus in the key topics most frequently addressed in standards; clearly local conditions may vary, but English language arts teachers across the country face many common challenges as they help students meet higher literacy standards. These first releases in the Standards Consensus Series draw on these common threads and bring together the best teaching ideas from prior NCTE publications in topical books with practical, everyday applications in the classroom. Among the titles available:

Teaching the Writing Process in High School (ISBN 0-8141-5286-4)
Stock No. 52864-4025
$12.95 nonmembers, $9.95 NCTE members

Teaching Literature in High School: The Novel (ISBN 0-8141-5282-1)
Stock No. 52821-4025
$12.95 nonmembers, $9.95 NCTE members

Teaching Literature in Middle School: Fiction (ISBN 0-8141-5285-6)
Stock No. 52856-4025
$12.95 nonmembers; $9.95 NCTE members

Motivating Writing in Middle School (ISBN 0-8141-5287-2)
Stock No. 52872-4025
$12.95 nonmembers, $9.95 NCTE members